THE
WITNESS

THE
WITNESS

NICOLA TALLANT

m
B
MIRROR BOOKS

First published by Mirror Books in 2020

Mirror Books is part of Reach plc
10 Lower Thames Street
London EC3R 6EN

www.mirrorbooks.co.uk

Print ISBN 978-1-913406-09-7
eBook ISBN: 978-1-913406-10-3

Typeset by Danny Lyle

Printed and bound in Great Britain by
CPI Group (UK) Ltd, Croydon, CR0 4YY

A CIP catalogue record for this book is available from the British Library.

Every effort has been made to fulfil requirements with regard to
reproducing copyright material. The author and publisher will be
glad to rectify any omissions at the earliest opportunity.

1 3 5 7 9 10 8 6 4 2

Cover credits: Adam Hirons/Millennium Images, UK

I would like to dedicate this book to my daughter K and my son Josh, I am so proud of you both and love you with every inch of my being. My amazing sisters; I can never show how much you mean to me, but I hope you know that I love you so much. Denis, thank you for supporting me and for being there for Ma.

And to you Ma; thank you, thank you, thank you! I wouldn't be here today if it wasn't for you. You dragged me from the depths of hell and showed me that there was a life worth living. You told me I could do it. You stood up for me when the world turned its back on me. You fought for me when no one else would and most of all you believed in me. You are the best mother in the world and I'm so lucky and grateful to have you in my life. I love you more than you will ever know, and, yes Ma, you are my hero. This book is for you.

Love your son Joseph xx

ABOUT THE AUTHOR

Nicola Tallant is the foremost authority on gangland crime in Ireland and holds an H Dip in Criminology.

A journalist for 20 years she is three times winner of the prestigious Newsbrands Crime Journalist of the Year Award and currently holds the title.

In her role as Investigations Editor of the Sunday World newspaper she has broken countless crime exclusives, delved into the darkest corners of the underworld and come face to face with some of the most notorious gangland criminals.

She is a regular contributor to television and radio programmes where she is called upon for her expertise about organised crime and has presented and produced a number of documentaries.

Nicola is the author of a number of books about crime, cults and murder. She has a particular interest in organised crime.

CHAPTER 1

**"I see Seven Towers.
But I only see one way out."**

My story really began well before I was even born, but in piecing together the jigsaw of my life I have come to realise that birth is a lottery and fate a hand of cards.

Ma came from, what we call in Dublin, "good stock." She was from a relatively wealthy family who could afford to live in a big red brick house in Ranelagh – still one of the most well-to-do suburbs of the city and where you were expected to marry well and prosper.

I often go there now and look at those big Victorian houses and wonder what it must have been like and how different her life was from mine. She talks really posh and has a gentle voice. She rarely curses and when she does it sounds so funny that it makes me and my sisters laugh. She's always called me "Joseph" even though most people used to call me "Joey". I speak a bit different than Ma, definitely more Dublin, but I don't have a very heavy accent either, nothing like me Da used to have.

Ma hated school and she would only realise later in life that she was dyslexic, a condition not recognised in the 1960s in Ireland. By the time she was a teenager she went to work in a hairdresser's and later in a department store in the centre of town called Roches Stores, where she met me Da. He was almost 10 years older than her and she remembers how he charmed her the minute she laid eyes on him.

Da was different to Ma and even as a child I seemed to know that. His name was Noel O'Callaghan and he came from Stoneybatter, a working class area of the inner city. His own ma, my Nanny O'Callaghan, was 48 years old when she had him and if that seems old now it must have been ancient back then. From what I can gather she had suffered a hard life at the hands of my granda who was regularly described as "fond of the gargle."

Ma's parents hated me Da from the minute they laid eyes on him, thinking he was too rough for their daughter. They were probably right. Ma was always very shy and mild mannered so I can only imagine what she was like back then. At 18 she was already pregnant with my oldest brother Patrick when she told her parents she was getting married. Back in 1975, in Catholic Ireland, unmarried women were sent to live in Magdalen laundries run by nuns if their fella got them pregnant and they brought shame on their own families. Ma's parents were devout and never missed Mass, so it was a sure sign of just how much they hated me Da when they called her aside on the morning of the wedding and whispered, "Mary you don't have to do this."

Ma married him anyway, despite the get-out-of-jail card, but I suppose she hoped she could change him. Like his own father, me Da was "fond of the gargle." Well he was maybe a bit more than fond of it. He drank beer from the minute he got up in the morning until he went to bed at night. There was always a can open and always a supply in the fridge, but I can never remember him going to a pub..

While I was too young to remember the violence, I know now that he used to beat Ma black and blue on a regular basis.

After the wedding, Ma had moved in with me Da to Nanny O'Callaghan's house. I never knew her, but Da talked about her often. She had some role in 1916, one of the women who went out and fought the British during the Rising, he said. I've had plenty of time to contemplate my past over the last few years so I often wandered up behind Manor Street to look at those houses and imagine what it must have been like. Most of them are modernised now and the area has become a bit hipster but back then it must have been very different.

The houses were built at the turn of the century by the Dublin Artisan Dwellings Company, which was a private body established by a group of investors. They included the very wealthy Guinness family, who are still spoken about in the city as wonderful employers who did all they could to relieve the conditions the poor were living in.

The "Artisans", as they became known, were fitted with a metal boot-scraper for working men to clean their shoes after a hard day's labour – some of the houses still have it, but it's retro now rather than functional. When they were built, the Artisans had no bathrooms but they were still a huge improvement for the hundreds of large families, often of 10 or more children, that squeezed into them. By the time Ma got there, most of them had been modernised. My Nanny's, however, still relied on a coal fire for heating and boiling water.

Within months of their marriage, Nanny O'Callaghan passed away and me Da inherited the house along with its mortgage.

Patrick was born in 1976, but Ma would now say that the realities of life with me Da had already lost any charm. Da was a "Provo" and very proud of it. He saw himself as an IRA hardman with Republican blood in his veins, and that gave him all the purpose in life he needed. He never held down a job, and while Ma stayed home he would spend his days at the bookies or hanging around with his Provo pals, boasting about how Nanny O'Callaghan had shot at British soldiers at the GPO. Reality never interfered with the drama of me Da's stories – and the fact that she would have only been a teenager at the time didn't seem to make her role any less important than the actual signatories of the Proclamation of Independence.

CHAPTER 1

I still find it hard to think of the things that me Da did to Ma, because he must have given her an awful life. Ma remembers three occasions when he tried to smother her as she lay asleep. Once, she says, she woke up to find him lying on top of her, his hands around her neck. On another occasion he struck her with a hot poker and smashed a cup right into her face. She tried to lock him out, to fight back, to play dead – but nothing worked. The beatings were constant, she has since told me, and I can vividly imagine now how her muffled screams must have been heard at night out on those Stoneybatter streets, as soon as he'd got in from wherever he'd been.

Ma is real gentle and everybody loves her. I'm sure she kept hoping he'd change but that's a lesson many of us learn the hard way.

While he beat her up, he spent all their money on drink and gambling. In 1978 my sister Niamh was born, followed by Louise nine months later. She was born premature and they have forever been known as the "Irish twins". With no heating and often no coal in the house, Ma says she had to wrap my brother and sisters in blankets to protect them against the cold, while me Da returned home drunk and sucking on bottles of Guinness.

Ma went out to work as soon as she could. She has always worked. I remember at one point she had three jobs working as a cleaner, a hairdresser and behind the counter of a sweet shop when we were only small. As a child you just take things for granted, but as an adult I'm proud of her now, and I can understand what it takes to do that under those circumstances.

Ma's parents must have felt really sorry for her. She told me she used to visit them every Saturday, and when it was time to go home they'd pack up a bag of food for her and hang it off the pram. Then Granda would slip her a few pounds. But me Da got cute to it, she says, and when she got home he'd be waiting for her in the hallway demanding the cash. She said she'd try and hide a bit so she could buy coal or food later in the week, depending on the time of year. It must have been miserable. He'd go out and drink her money and then when he came home he'd punch her, throw her against the walls and punish her for nothing.

Ma says she got a call one day from a bank, saying she was being evicted and they were coming to take the house. It turned out that me Da had bought it with Nanny O'Callaghan off the local authority, but after she died he hadn't made any repayments. And that was it, Ma had to go – and no amount of begging would change the situation.

Pregnant with John Paul and with three small children, Ma turned to the Dublin Corporation and declared herself homeless, begging them to house her anywhere they could in the city. It must have been just another comedown from the splendour of her childhood, but she still says she was very grateful when a flat became available on Sillogue Road, after a young woman and her family were transferred out of it. So that is how Ma and me Da got to Ballymun, a place I still love and hate in equal measure today.

Ballymun had been launched in a blaze of promise, but by the time Ma and me Da got there it had gone spectacularly wrong. In the 1960s its pre-fabricated "system building" was celebrated as the answer to a housing crisis in the city, which had become pressing after the collapse of two tenements and the resulting deaths of elderly residents and children. Mass panic had engulfed Dublin after that, as fears grew that buildings housing large families were dangerous and needed to be demolished before they fell down on their own. The Dublin Corporation was becoming overwhelmed with the volume of requests for housing and something needed to be done quickly.

Set out in blocks of four to 15 stories in height, and providing more than 3,000 homes for 12,000 people in just over four years, Ballymun was hailed as the answer to the issues facing the housing authorities.

Artists' impressions of the new town showed happy children in playgrounds, adults strolling with pushchairs around tree-lined pavements, cars parked in neat rows and clean modern living in the towers above. High rise social housing was nothing new in Europe but this was a first for Ireland and the speed with which it got underway was said to have been incredible.

50 years after the 1916 Easter Rising it was decided that the towers would be named after the seven signatories of the Proclamation of Independence – such was their importance

in Ireland's history. Patrick Pearse Tower was the first of the high rises to be completed in 1966.

Things started to go wrong as soon as the ribbons had been cut on Ballymun's launch. Across the water a gas explosion would mark the beginning of the end for high rise buildings like Ballymun's Seven Towers. The explosion, I read, in 1968, collapsed Ronan Point in London, leaving four people dead and 17 injured. The disaster at the 22-storey tower block led to major changes in the UK's building regulations. Despite one sixth of its local authority housing being high-rise at that time, the British Government reversed its building plans and had decided by 1974 that no more tower blocks would be built. In Paris, the government had already banned similar housing projects, describing them as "inhumane".

In Ballymun by the mid-1970s, the sparkle was gone. Constant problems with the lift system inside the towers had made life unbearable for many. There were tales of young mothers being forced to drag bags of shopping, buggies and small children up concrete stairwells to their isolated homes on the top floors.

Less than a decade after building had begun, experts were warning that the Ballymun complex was "disastrous" and that problems were likely to "explode" as its population of 8,000 children got older.

The flats had been filled with families from all over the city, but amenities like a swimming pool, a dance hall, a bowling alley, restaurants and shops were never built, and the town centre turned out far grimmer than the artists had visualised. Instead of a tree-lined town centre there was a dull shopping centre, shaped like a crucifix, with a pub at each end. It was in The Towers Pub, which was nicknamed "The Penthouse", where Ballymun drowned its sorrows with gusto.

And of course, there was the heroin… because it was outside the flats, in the common areas and on the graffiti-covered stairwells, where Ballymun's biggest problem was laid bare.

Despite what was happening outside, inside our three-bed flat must have been absolute luxury for Ma. Compared to the crumbling Artisan off Manor Street it was heaven. It not only had running water and a flushing loo, but also some heat for a winter's night. She could wash her kids in a bath and she was nearer her own parents' home, too.

Ma always says she didn't care about the reputation of Ballymun – to her it was nirvana compared to her previous abode. She says she was grateful too that my brother John Paul was born healthy, as Da was in a particularly violent phase during her pregnancy. He had beaten her almost every day and had dragged her by the hair down a flight of stairs in her final trimester.

In the winter of 1985, Ma made her way to the Rotunda Hospital where, on January 26, she gave birth to me, her fifth child. While, by order of birth, I would become me Da's favourite and was spared his wrath, Ma says it hadn't looked that way from the beginning. She would later tell me that when Da drunkenly made his way into the hospital, he was far from happy. Swaying at the end of Ma's bed he belched, and looking down into the cot at me, announced, "It's definitely not mine" before nursing staff had to remove him from the ward.

By the time she got home I think Ma must have been a broken woman. Despite being just 28 she had already endured a decade of violence at the hands of me Da and nursing a new baby gave her no respite. The beatings started up again immediately, almost as soon as she got through the front door. Ma says she was thrilled with me despite her circumstances but as I have drilled back into my past I have realised that she did well to keep going at all.

After I was born she says that she did find it more difficult to cope. I think that Da was getting more and more violent and she was just getting fed up of being his punch bag. She says that at the time she blamed it on how cramped the flat was, filled with five children descending in height like a flight of stairs. She was tired dragging us all up and down the stairs and she said she longed for a house with a small garden where she could throw open the doors and let the older ones out to play. She laughs now when she remembers how she thought a house with a door and a bit of grass would make everything better. When a neighbour told her to fill in a housing application to find a three-bed rather than a four-bed house, she got lucky and soon found herself moved up the waiting list.

CHAPTER 1

Clearly I have no memory of it but I do know that when I was 18 months we got our first house, just ten minutes from Ballymun flats, in a place called Poppintree. Ma says she was thrilled but as soon as she moved in she realised that the house wasn't the issue – she could no longer cope with me Da's violence. Even as a single mother of five, life must have seemed more hopeful without him. She says that not long after we moved and following a series of severe beatings, she somehow found some courage and made her way to the courts to obtain a barring order against me Da. A few Gardai accompanied her back to the house and removed him from the property, warning him he would be jailed if he tried to approach Ma again.

I was oblivious to it all as I was just learning to crawl, but I'm sure it was all very dramatic. Ma still says I was a lovely little baby and that I was always smiling from ear to ear. She says that people used to stop her on the street to admire me and my blonde curls. While she thought the barring order would keep us all safe, it didn't stop me Da from showing up at all hours of the night. Ma says she had to constantly call the Gardai on him and eventually she got so fed up she decided to move to England and try to make a life there.

In desperation to get away from him, she says, she agreed to give him the house in Poppintree and let the children choose which parent they wanted to be with. The boys moved in with Da while Ma left, hoping never to return. Within a year, however, pregnant with number six, she was back in Dublin and having to declare herself homeless. We got another flat in Ballymun and my little sister Natalie was born.

I was still only small but I can vividly remember feeling fear. Sometimes Ma would have male visitors and me Da would show up red with rage. There were big blow ups and then periods of calm but there was always tension. I remember one day sitting at the dinner table and complaining because there was turnip on my plate. There was a man at the table who I didn't like. The food was orange and I said it looked like my cordial drink in the glass in front of me. He flipped, picked up the glass and poured the orange squash all over my dinner. Then he smashed my face over and over again into the plate until the food was in my eyes, up my nose and in my hair. On another occasion I remember someone beating Ma and I t attacked him, trying to stop him. I was pulling at his legs trying to get him off her. It was Christmas time and the flat was decorated. He picked me up by the back of my neck and hurled me across the room into the tree. I was so worried I had ruined Christmas and that Santa would see what I had done.

Ma told me in recent years about the crushing guilt she always feels for bringing violence to our home and for the choices she made when she was younger. Ma isn't stupid but she certainly must have been naïve when she believed time and again that each time a man beat her, it would be the last.

CHAPTER 1

I think I was about six when Ma decided she needed some escape from it all. She threw herself into work and the pub so she could avoid the reality of the life awaiting her in the flat. Tormented by her bad choices and desperate situation as a single mother of six, she started drinking heavily. My only real memories around that time were that she was never there. She was always working or out and when she was around, Niamh and Louise would be telling me to be quiet and not wake her up. I wasn't to know she was hungover and when I think of myself as a small child I can still feel a terrible emptiness there.

I was often very scared. Ma's only role in our lives seemed to be to provide food for the cupboards. Natalie and me never appreciated it but she had pretty much left Niamh and Louise to assume the role of our parents. She never dropped or collected me from school. The girls would get us ready in the morning, give us our breakfast at the table, and give us a packed lunch. Then they'd walk us off to school and collect us again and do our homework and get us our tea until we were old enough to do it ourselves. I remember often at night the girls bundling us up in warm coats and bringing us with them to the Towers pub where they would draw odds on who had to go in to beg Ma to come home. One of my earliest memories is of being frightened and stepping over the bodies of the junkies on the landings at night time as we made our way back to the flat. When she was home Ma was cranky. Some nights I recall the ambulance coming and being pushed into my room where I would listen to the muffled appeals of fire officers begging her to stay awake while they got her to hospital. I didn't know what was going on, but I knew I wasn't safe.

Somehow Ma managed to hold down a job throughout her breakdown. And looking back now I think that as long as she was working, she believed that drink wasn't a major problem in her life. Niamh and Louise were good to me. They were really only children themselves but they were strict and streetwise. They knew the dangers that lurked outside the flat. They rarely left me by myself but they had Natalie to look after as well and I managed to push the boundaries. Life in the flat was a bit of a merry go round with Ma staying off the drink for a time but then falling back into late nights and groggy mornings when we wouldn't see her and I would lie awake waiting to hear her key in the door. I think that's why I loved going to me Da's so much. He was still drinking but he always did it at home. He never went out much unless he had meetings to attend.

I adored me Da. Sitting on the doorstep cradled under his huge tattooed arm I would listen intently as he named off all the stars in the night sky and entertained me with stories of the brave Irish men who had risen up against their British oppressors. I loved spending weekends with me Da even though he lived only ten minutes away from our flat. While our separate family units may have seemed complex, it actually worked out quite well. For all that had gone on between them, Ma never stopped me going to see me Da and she never gave out about him. That was really big of her and it allowed me to have a great relationship with him. I saw him as a hero who was respected and feared in equal measures.

Da had a particular soft spot for me and I loved him back. On weekend visits or during his holidays I loved nothing more than the nod from me Da to hop up on the crossbar of his bike and the two of us would freewheel our way to Ballymun, stopping off at the off-licence. Da would buy cans of lager and a packet of Chewitts for me before making our way back to his house. He would allow me to play on the green outside while he stood in the doorway watching.

His house was bedecked in Republican memorabilia. The Irish tricolour: green, white and orange, hung in the sitting room and the kitchen. Plaques and posters to the martyrs of 1916 lined the walls. The Irish Proclamation of Independence, the signatories of which the rat-infested Towers were named after, hung in pride of place. His Republican comrades regularly met in the house, staying up late into the night banging their fists and shouting about a "United Ireland." I would hear them as I nodded off to sleep upstairs wrapped in an itchy woollen blanket.

I knew people were afraid of me Da. He would encourage my brothers to go out and fight and get stuck in if someone started an argument. Sometimes he would give them and my sisters a wallop but he never hit me. He'd say that they had to toughen up and that it was the only way to survive. I remember trying to reason that he only beat them when he had cause: if they were cheeky, or late or if he caught them smoking. It never, ever occurred to me that he shouldn't have hit them at all. In a way violence was so entrenched in our childhood that it had become normalised. Me Da would also encourage me to know how to fight my corner should the need arise. Other kids often approached me and told me stories about me Da running "pushers" out of the flats or spray-painting the windows of people's homes. Nobody messed with Noel O'Callaghan, and in a way that gave me street credit too.

He hated the junkies and he'd often stand on the doorstep and shout at them if they came anywhere near his house. "Yiz better fuck off, yiz dirty bastards," he'd roar at them and make them go the long way round if they wanted to pass. Ma was a bit more compassionate about them and used to tell us to feel sorry for them. "They are sick Joseph, don't be staring at them." I was well used to them. In a way they were as much a part of my childhood as being flung through the air into a Christmas tree. When I was younger I believed the men and women with the skinny frames and the gaunt sunken faces who hung around on the stairwells were hungry. As I got older, I knew them as junkies and was aware that they looked the way they did because of drugs.

By the time I was seven or eight I was well used to watching gangs of them standing around the green areas and waiting for a car to pull up. People used to joke that Ballymun's junkies were nearly as famous as Bono, who had penned U2's iconic song "Running to Stand Still" about them. The song, released on the band's 1987 *Joshua Tree* album, tells the story of a heroin addict seeing just "one way out" of Ballymun when she "suffers the needle chill." As me and other kids played football or chase we would watch the junkies moving like a herd towards their dealer when he arrived in what looked like a really fancy car. He would inevitably reach down the back of his tracksuit pants and retrieve what I knew as smack. Some of us kids would giggle when one would make a comment about taking it out of his bum. I thought that was a joke back then but in later years I realised that was indeed where the little bags were coming from. Once they were produced there would be a flurry of exchanges before the dealer would retreat back to his car and the junkies would scatter towards the seven towers. We'd forget about them for a while and continue with our games but sometimes we'd see them returning to the large open spaces wide-eyed and dazed. It might have been an intriguing sight for many but for us it was perfectly normal.

Needles littered the stairwells of the flats and sometimes me and my friends would have a bit of fun by kicking our ball against bins near the junkies and watching them jump with the noise. We'd then run off in hoots of laughter. Some would stagger over towards us and whine, "got any gear", but we'd run away, afraid of catching "the virus" off them.

I didn't really know what that was, "the virus." I thought it was just some condition that was part of being a junkie, like having a cough or a sneeze and that if I got too close I could catch it and turn into one of them. Mostly they walked around like zombies who seemed to either love or hate the world. I'd often see them fighting with one another over money or "gear". Often at night I could hear other people fighting too. Through the walls I'd hear the women scream-ing and begging, just as Ma had.

Growing up in the 1980s and early 1990s in Ballymun you simply couldn't miss the devastation that the heroin epidemic caused. Needles lay everywhere and as children we picked our way over the unconscious bodies of drug addicts. The stench of urine seeped into the concrete blocks in the stairwells which had started to fracture and crack. Horses wandered the wastelands where playing pitches should have been built before the government funding ran dry. The experts can see now how it happened and why Ballymun was one of the worst hit areas with its massive unemployment, lack of amenities and the sense of hopelessness that hung in the air but back then nobody seemed to care. Nobody except for me Da and his mates that is.

Da's hatred of the "junkies" went far beyond just shout-ing at the sick skeletons that moved through our community focused on their next fix. He absolutely despised them and often threatened them with baseball bats or other weapons if they came near him. "Never hit a junkie with yer fists son, ye could get the virus," he'd tell me. He hated the dealers or the pushers even more. What I didn't know then was that when me Da and his friends marched on a drug dealer's home with their banners ordering them to "Get Out" or when they beat up some junkies trying to sell smack to kids they were part of something far greater than just cleaning up Ballymun. "I'm a Concerned Parent," he'd tell me, pausing to let that sink in before he would aggressively continue, "I won't have me son looking at these filthy junkies. They won't come near me family with the virus. We'll run them out." Then he'd crack open another beer.

Everyone lived on top of one another in the concrete jungle that was home. We called it the Bronx and we had to keep our wits about us. Even as a young child I had witnessed first-hand how quickly you could go downhill from drugs. One girl that our family knew had literally transformed in front of my eyes in a few short months. This tall, blonde and Barbie doll-like teenager had dazzled me when I first laid eyes on her at a relative's house. I didn't think I had ever seen anyone so beautiful. I remember Louise laughing at me. "Jesus, Joey, close yer mouth or you'll catch a fly." I was embarrassed I'd been caught staring and my cheeks reddened. I think I was kind of in love with her but then I heard she was using smack and one day when I was walking across the fields to me Da's house I saw her emerging from a bush pulling her trousers up.

She had those same hollowed cheeks as the junkies and her hair was limp and greasy, her clothing stained and her arms covered in marks. I stopped dead in my tracks and tried to say hello to her but nothing came out of my mouth and although I stood right in front of her she didn't seem to see me.

"And Da," I gasped, when I got to Poppintree. "I saw three men zipping up their trousers coming out of the bush behind her. They looked like they were doin' their wee. Is tha' wha' they were doin, Da? Are they the junkies too?" Da took a huge swig of his beer and shook his head dramatically before opening the door and shouting out onto the street, "Fuckin' scumbag junkie slut. Me son shouldn't have to see tha'. Scumbags! Junkies! Sluts." He walked down as far as the front gate and continued roaring up the road. I was mortified and vowed never to ask me Da about anything like that again. While I had no idea what slut meant, I knew all the rest and decided I didn't need to ask questions again.

I was witnessing through a child's eyes one of the greatest social issues of our time. Heroin had first been introduced to Dublin by an entrepreneurial criminal called Larry Dunne in the late 1970s, showing up first in the north and south inner cities and quickly spreading its tentacles outwards like a cancer. Dunne had taken advantage of the mass exodus of business-man from Iran after the Revolution, who fled the country after exchanging their cash for heroin. As the Ayatollah Khomeini overthrew the Shah, hundreds of once rich Iranians made

CHAPTER 1

their way to Europe where they exchanged their heroin back into cash, resulting in an enormous glut of the drug on the market. Dunne had seen the potential of the drug and back home he started to sell it to impoverished communities. Quickly it flowed into flat complexes and housing estates at a time when there was no work for anyone and even the jobs down at the docks, which had provided vast employment for the working classes, were gone. Of course back then I didn't even know where Iran was let alone the significance of the political unrest there. I didn't have a clue what me Da meant when he talked about being a "Concerned Parent Against Drugs". But I'd later realise that the movement was a huge part of the working class response to the flood of smack all the way from the Persian Gulf.

The CPAD, as they were known, had been born out of desperation. Within years of its arrival, heroin, the spread of HIV and the resulting deaths of kids in huge numbers began to cause massive social problems. The movement had started in the north inner city just two years before I was born. At the vast Hardwicke Street flats complex, a Jesuit priest, Fr Jim Smyth, brought together politicians and locals at open air meetings to discuss the heroin problem and they decided that pushers would be approached and asked to stop selling smack. The campaign quickly spread across the city and into other badly effected complexes like St Theresa's Gardens.. The Hardwicke Street flats, where one of the founding members, John 'Whacker' Humphries, was from, had been a major centre of drug dealing where up to 200 addicts a day went for their fix. By the time I was lying in my cot in the Rotunda Hospital locals around the corner were telling reporters from the national broadcaster, RTE, that they had stamped out smack dealing through their own CPAD policing. The innocence of such statements is forever captured on those old reports.

As the movement grew it started to become pretty famous and gained in confidence. In 1983, when I was just three years old, a study was released called the Bradshaw Report which found that in one area of Dublin, around the north inner city's Sean McDermott Street, 15% of young people under 25 were on heroin. The statistics proved that parts of Dublin had bigger problems than New York's Harlem. But the CPAD were there where the politicians weren't. Marches were organised on the homes of the big drug dealers of the time like Tony King Scum Felloni. He had been nick-named by the media as his policy was to keep the business within the family by turning his own kids into addicts so they would work for him. He was so greedy that he dealt directly to street pushers. He got very rich until the pressure put on the government and police by the people like me Da in the CPAD resulted in the Gardai setting up the undercover detectives known as the Mockeys. Articles from 1986 report that the Mockeys hid outside Felloni's home at Palmerstown

Place and watched him remove a black sock from the garden shed. They found thousands of pounds worth of heroin in it and a further stash of £100k in his flat. He was sentenced to 10 years in court and as he was led away to prison, members of the CPAD cheered and applauded.

In another incident a coffin was left outside Thomas Boxer Mullens' house and he was named in the Irish parliament under Dail privilege which gives politicians the legal protection to say pretty much anything they want without getting sued. Larry Dunne in particular was challenged by the group as he was believed to be the first to bring heroin to the city. His nickname was Flash Larry because he lived in a mansion high in the Dublin mountains and travelled around the city in a chauffeur-driven limo. He was put on trial in 1983 but absconded and was convicted in his absence. Two years later he was arrested in Portugal and returned to Ireland. When he was jailed for drug trafficking he shouted from his prison van, "If you thought we were bad, just wait 'till you see what's coming next." This prophetic statement would be quoted for years to come and would become very significant in my own future life.

Articles from the newspapers at the time about the CPAD and their activities along with bulletins I have watched online show these highly-charged marches on the homes of suspected dealers. Many of the protesters interviewed had lost loved ones to heroin and had watched as their neighbourhoods had been destroyed by the drug. As the years went by it was claimed the

IRA had latched on to the CPAD and were providing them with security to challenge the pushers. But at the same time, some experts now say, the IRA were using it as a recruitment vehicle to set up a system of vigilante-style policing within those same communities. I remember that me Da's identity was certainly caught up in two things – being a Provo and a Concerned Parent - but I don't think he was very politically aware. I imagine it was his fists rather than his brain which motivated him to get involved, and looking back now, I think that for him, on a basic level, it was a way of making him feel better about himself.

Ballymun was crazy and in its own way it was a bit like the Serengeti with predators everywhere. As a child you needed your Ma and your Da. I didn't really have either because they were too caught up in their own problems and their addictions. While the dealers looked out for vulnerable kids without the protection of a Da like Noel O'Callaghan or the Provos, there were also others watching in the close and confined living quarters. And I was often alone, a child on the landings playing with my *Star Wars* figures. Unbeknownst to me the man in the neighbouring block was collecting figurines too. And when he'd collected enough he invited me to his flat one day to play with his toys. I remember going with him and I remember the door closing, slamming shut.

Da wasn't around then to act tough and to put his huge arm around me. He was at home with his cans of beer and his songs of Ireland. Ma wasn't there either. She was out working – one of her three jobs or in the pub drowning her sorrows. But the girls came looking for me, Niamh and Louse, still only children themselves. I remember they were like lionesses looking for their cub but they were too late and something awful had happened. I didn't understand at the time but I knew that what the man did to me was wrong and I knew when the girls battered down the door to get to me that they were angry and upset. I remember watching them as they raged and attacked him, kicking and punching him before his own parents, an elderly couple, intervened. There was lots of screaming as they took me away. "You fuckin' pervert, stay away from me little brudder," I remember Niamh roaring over her shoulder as she led me away. And then life went on because Ballymun was a bit like that. Nobody cared. You just had to get up, dust yourself down and get on with things. Shit happened – all the time.

CHAPTER 2

From the minute she met Niall, Ma was a completely different person. I can clearly remember the change being both instant and dramatic. It was like she had awoken. Instead of being absent or ill-tempered she was at home and nice, and even as a young child I knew that somehow Niall had saved her. I was wary of him at first but I needn't have been. Niall was caring, jovial and good-humoured. He was quick to smile and we all warmed to him. He drove a taxi and while he had two sons of his own from a previous relationship, he had lots of time for me and the girls. Relating to children came naturally to him and we always felt included. There was never any suggestion, however, that he was taking on a father's role for me and while I was happy for him to be around I kept him at arm's length emotionally.

Although Niall was never going to be my saviour there is no doubt that meeting him drew Ma out of the hopeless place she had been in. She started dressing nice and got a promotion in the cleaning company she worked for. I remember distinctly that when she was offered a company car with this new managerial role, Niall set out to teach her how to drive. I watched them with so much glee from my bedroom window where I could just about see out towards the back of the flats. I strained my neck to see the taxi jerk and stutter across the ground below until it eventually began making smoother progress. Very quickly we made leaps up the social ladder. Instead of being the O'Callaghan kids who had less than the other children in the flats, I found myself dressed for the first time in Ben Sherman shirts and Wrangler jeans, then considered the height of designer fashion, and enjoying days out to Bray seafront for bags of chips. From time to time Ma and Niall would even take us children out for a meal. I felt like the cat who had got the cream.

While I could see they got on, I didn't realise back then that one of the things that had brought Niall and Ma together was their shared desire to get us kids away from the flats and away from the junkies and the smack. Ballymun really was bad and it was only getting worse. It wasn't at all unusual at that time to walk in or out of our flat to find two junkies having sex outside or going to the toilet on the landings. Smack is a filthy drug and everything about it is unhygienic and encroaching. While I seemed to just take it all with a grain of salt, Niall and Ma had both had enough and they were saving hard in order to get us the hell out. Eventually the time came.

I remember the night they told us that we were moving. I was 11 years old and I think it was the worst night of my whole life. Niall and Ma had called us all in to the sitting room to tell us their big news. Louise and Niamh clearly knew all about it in advance because when they told us they had bought a house in Blanchardstown and we'd be moving, the girls didn't even flinch. I, on the other hand, thought I was going to collapse and I felt my stomach cave in my body and my mouth hang open. "It's a gorgeous house and we won't know ourselves for all the space we will have," Ma told us. "We've bought the house. It's ours and look – we have the keys and all." She held up her hand and dangled two little keys from a ring, looking from one to the other of us. She must have seen the horror on my face because she went on, albeit with less confidence, to tell us about the garden out the back and the big green pitches nearby and how I was going to have my own bedroom. "Joseph, you are going to just love it. Wait until ye see all the kids your age that live there. And there are proper football pitches where ye can play." Niall held her hand and I glared at him. It was very unlike me to act up but in my childish head I was sure that I could see exactly what was going on. I just knew that Niall was trying to take me away from me Da. "We'll be moving tomorrow. So yiz might want to pack up yer things," he said, trying to jolly the situation along. There was silence in the flat and everyone looked at me sensing the tension.

"I'm not goin' anywhere with 'yiz. I'm stayin' here," I remember roaring, more at Niall than Ma. "I know exactly what yiz are doing and I'm not goin' with yiz. Yiz can fuck off to Blanchardstown all yiz want. I'm stayin' here." Then I got up. bolted for the door and like a greyhound took off down the four flights of stairs, vaulting over a junkie with a needle in her arm and out onto the park toward Poppintree. When I arrived at me Da's my cheeks were burning and I was gulping for breath. Da brought me into the kitchen and sat me down, turning to take a beer from the fridge as he waited to hear what was wrong. The familiar hiss of the cap as he cracked open the can of Dutch Gold gave me an odd comfort that I can still feel today. Between gasps for breath I told him about the "dreadful news" and the plan to move to some place whose name I couldn't even remember, and where I told him I would be totally and utterly miserable. "I'm not goin'. No way J-O-S-E. Not if they pay me." Confidently, I recall completing the story with the announcement that I would be moving in with me Da. He gulped down the beer in one go and opened the fridge for another. "Now Joe, I'm gonna ring yer Ma and have a little chat about all dis," he said. The fresh can hissed as he lit a cigarette and stared at me intently.

It was probably the first time I had ever known me Da use the phone supplied in his council house. For as long as I could remember, if anyone ever needed to contact him they had to ring a neighbour's house and he'd then be told there was a call for him. I had never understood his aversion to using his own phone but he was always going on about the cops listening in on his calls. "Mary, it's Noel. I've Joe here with me," I heard him say, then he closed the kitchen door and walked out of my earshot, can in hand. I tiptoed to the door and stuck my ear to it to try to hear what he was saying. There was a muffled conversation from which I could only make out a few bits and eventually I heard him saying, "You fuckin' talk to him den." I leapt back into my chair as the kitchen door swung open and me Da motioned for me to go to the phone.

On the end of the line Ma sounded worried. She promised that I could continue to see me Da when we moved to Blanchardstown and that I would be really happy there. She told me again all about the huge house and about all the kids that were there for me to play with on the estate. She told me that I would love my new home and my new school and that I would have a fabulous bedroom all to myself. "Joseph, it's a new start for all of us. I'm doing this for you and for Natalie. We need a new start."

As me Da tucked me in under the itchy blanket that night, I felt exhausted from the tears and the wailing and the begging that had continued for hours. I didn't sleep immediately. Instead I lay awake and smelt the cigarette smoke wafting up the stairs and listened to the sounds of me Da's voice rising and falling in the kitchen below. His house mightn't have been a palace but it was always there for me and everything about it was familiar. I was filled with a dreadful sense of foreboding. While Ballymun was hell to many, to us all it was home, a place where we knew our neighbours, flaws and all.

The drive to Blanchardstown was the loneliest journey I could have ever imagined. Nothing looked familiar. The back roads were still pretty rural then, even though Blanchardstown had already been growing outwards for two decades from what was once a small rural village to the largest urban area of north Dublin. Despite the massive developments that had occurred, the road network hadn't kept up. And although construction was well underway on the M50 motorway which would eventually sweep around Dublin and make Blanchardstown much more accessible, it hadn't been completed. So instead of being a short trip like it is now from Ballymun, getting to Blanchardstown seemed to take forever. In the back seat of the car I looked out at the passing fields and ditches as my home was left far, far behind.

There was no doubt but the house was beautiful. It was on an estate called Ashmount and it had little driveway at the front with gates and pillars. As I child I thought there was a big turret on top but it was really just the design of the house, with two bay windows to the front and a smaller window above the front door. Inside there was a long hallway and two sitting rooms with a kitchen to the back overlooking a garden. There were four bedrooms upstairs and I was allocated mine – the box room to the front of the house. Ma helped me put my stuff away and tried to cajole me along about all the new friends I was going to make, but I still had a heavy heart.

Despite all me Da's promises that he would come and see me, I knew that would never happen. Da didn't go anywhere other than down to the off-licence and off to his meetings with his pals. More often than not people came to him. I couldn't ever remember him getting a bus or going to town, let alone travelling to the middle of nowhere which was where I felt my new neighbourhood was. For the first few weeks everything was new and there was a good bit of exploring to do but even though I got used to it, I didn't settle in. I yearned for home and I worked out the bus route to Ballymun which took more than an hour and a half. Nonetheless, I made my way cross country to see me Da whenever I could, staying overnight and dreading when the time came to go back.

At the new school I was teased mercilessly. I was tiny, by far the smallest in my class and that certainly didn't help. Kids told me to go back to the flats and they nicknamed me Ballymun. The more the word got around the worse it got. I tried to keep my head down but it was relentless. They chanted at me as I walked through the corridors. "There goes Ballymun. Be careful. He'll rob your runners," they'd say before the whole school seemed to erupt into mocking laughter. In the classroom they whispered and threw notes onto my desk with names and rude drawings scrawled on them. Sometimes groups would fall silent as I passed by, only to explode into fits of giggles behind my back. I was miserable and lonely and felt as if my whole life had ended. The rest of the family seemed to be faring much better. Louise had joined the army and was due to go on a tour of duty to Lebanon, while Niamh had got a job locally and started dating fairly quickly. Natalie seemed to be settling in but I was afraid that she was going to get targeted in school too and I looked out for her in the yard. "You come to me now if anyone says anything to ye. Do ye hear me?" I'd say to her each morning as we made our way in.

One day I was furious when I found Natalie crying in the yard. "He, he tried to take me Walkman," she told me, clutching her recorder and pointing towards a corner where she indicated the boy had gone. "Don't say nuttin', Joey. He's real big." The Walkman was Natalie's pride and joy and had been her Christmas present from Santa. It weighed on her like a heavy yoke and ate batteries, but she had treated it with the utmost care since she got it. I was furious. It was like everything got on top of me and I could hear me Da's voice telling me to "get in there son." Filled with rage I grabbed the big clunky recorder from Natalie's hand and rounded the corner to confront her tormentor, only to be greeted by a hulking traveller known as Big Tommy standing in front of me. He had orange hair and translucent-white skin. He was covered in freckles and he looked down on me with a big grin plastered across his face. "What the fuck do you want Ballymun?" he mocked. As huge as Tommy was I somehow wasn't put off by his bulk and I still felt that surge of anger as I looked up at him and decided there was only one way. "You want this?" I roared as I brought the Walkman full-force upwards and smashed it into Big Tommy's face. Blood spurted from his nose and he wobbled backward, his size making him awkward and less agile than me. And then I kept smashing it. Over and over again while a crowd gathered and a silence descended on the yard. "You wanna know what Ballymun is like? This is what it's like ye prick, ye. Feel it now. Do you feel it now?" I didn't finish until I was pulled off him and frog-marched down to the office where I was ordered to stand in a corner while they rang home.

Ma wasn't pleased but I think she probably felt a bit sorry for me too because she knew they hadn't been nice to me at school. "What were you thinking Joseph?" she asked. "Do you want them to think that you are that kind of a boy?" I didn't care what they thought. Suspended, I was forced to stay home and my sense of isolation only increased. I spent days on end in Ballymun with me Da and when I came back to Blanchardstown I seemed to be even more lonely, depressed and miserable than ever. I know Ma was worried that I'd get bored and get into trouble but there wasn't much she could do. "I know you don't like school but things will get better, I promise," she'd say. I knew she hoped that the transition the following September into secondary school would help. "This is our home now, Joseph, and you will have to make an effort to make some friends." If the truth be told I think Ma was questioning the move to Blanchardstown herself. In Ballymun we had nothing, but Ma did at least have friends and neighbours who would watch me if she was at work. We looked out for one another but in Blanchardstown and in the new estate you hardly spoke to the people next door. It felt weird.

Despite the suspension, Ma managed to convince the principal to give me another chance and after a few weeks I reluctantly went back to school. Things weren't any better until I eventually made a friend. I have to admit that despite my overwhelming negativity since the move, I had been intrigued by the house across the road. The Coates were a huge family of 11 and they lived behind large gates in a massive house with a pond in the back garden. Through the gates I could see that the pond could be crossed via a bridge and it looked almost like something out of a fairy tale book. The father, Norman, had a car garage opposite the house, on our side of the road, and there were always people coming and going. I had gazed at the house for months and at the hordes of children and teenagers of all ages before plucking up the courage to go over one day and introduce myself to the boy who looked to be about the same height as me. "How're ye. I'm Joey," I said to him as I kicked a ball against the kerb. "Do ye want to play football?" The boy looked at me and smiled. "Adam," he said. "Ye. I'll play." Before I knew it we were chatting and kicking the ball together and talking about everything from our favourite football players to our brothers and sisters.

I honestly cannot remember which bit I found more exotic – the pond or the fact that Adam's older brother Shane was in prison, but I remember being just blown away by both. I came home that evening full of news about Adam and the fish in his garden but I had sense enough to omit the bit about the brother being in jail. We soon started to meet on the street where we played ball and chatted. Ma must have heard something about the family because while she was initially delighted that I'd made a friend she soon tried to discourage me from hanging out with Adam. In fact from very early on she warned me that I wasn't to go into the house and that she'd rather see me playing with other boys. "I'm just not comfortable with you hanging around there, Joseph. I want you to promise me you won't be going into that house." I guessed Ma must have heard about Shane but she was always at work so she didn't know that I was not only becoming a firm friend of Adam but that I had secured an invite to see the pond.

I remember to this day sitting on the bridge swinging our legs above the water as Adam told me all about Shane and his best pal Stephen, and the reputation the two of them had around Blanchardstown. They were like me Da multiplied by a million and they sounded very exciting. Looking back now it is ironic to think how unlucky Ma was when she moved to Blanchardstown and ended up living across the road from one of the most violent criminals that Dublin's underworld would ever see. While she and Niall had hoped their new home would allow us to escape from Ballymun and the heroin epidemic, in truth they had moved the family from the frying pan right into a raging fire. The 1980s might have been the decade defined by heroin and its effects on communities, but the 1990s had brought with it, as Flash Larry Dunne had prophesied, a new generation of drug dealers who were far more ruthless and ambitious than what had gone before them. Of the gangs of violent young criminals who had popped up across the city staking their claims on drug turf, none would define this new breed more terrifyingly than the mob led by Adam's brother Shane Coates and his pal Stephen Sugg, known in later years as the Westies.

Coates and Suggs were already top targets for the Gardai while still teenagers and had started their criminal careers stealing and joyriding cars. Adam used to tell me bits about their exploits, about the smash and grab raids and the like. "Wait until ye meet dem Joey, der mad tings. You'll luv dem." He didn't tell me that they had made the inevitable transition into drugs after their exploits with firearms and the like but I'd kind of worked that one out myself. I'd also worked out that it was their reputation for violence that ensured they stood out from the growing number of dangerous gangs populating Blanchardstown.

In fact shortly before we moved there, the Westies had been locked up when they came a cropper of the law. They had been caught while attempting to rob a butchers with a shotgun and were put away for what seemed like a long time. While I knew to keep my friendship with Adam a secret from Ma, I loved nothing better than sitting listening to him telling me all about his jailbird brother and his antics in prison. "He'd carve yer man up if he could," Adam would boast as I'd hang on his every word. We spent the summer together kicking ball and examining the fish, and back at school in September my friendship with Adam was well-noted. Nobody bullied me at all and everything seemed a little bit more bearable.

As the months wore on I had started to cut ties a bit with my old friends in Ballymun and maybe because I was getting that bit older I didn't feel that same wrench from me Da either. The bus journeys had all but stopped and when I did see him I seemed to be constantly making excuses about why I hadn't visited. "I'm busy Da, in school and dat," I'd say to him. The following January, just as I turned 12, Adam got fantastic news. A judge had decided to review some cases and had decided to let his big brother out. "Wait until ye meet him Joey, just wait," he told me. I was sick with excitement and felt like I'd managed to latch on to someone's VIP pass to meet a celebrity.

"Shane, dis is Joey, me friend," Adam said as he introduced me to his famous brother one afternoon. I could hardly look up and shifted my feet as I muttered, "How're ya". Shane nodded and hopped into a car telling Adam he would see him later. I could hardly believe my luck. Being friendly with Adam had undoubtedly helped my transition into secondary school but with Shane Coates out of jail I had found myself propelled to a stardom of my own. Now that he had nodded at me I was sure I would enjoy a whole new status in the school corridors. Immediately I got a bit of a spring in my step. From relying on me Da's reputation in Ballymun, I was now able to reply on Shane's in Blanchardstown . At home I'd sneak over to Adam's to play and was often there when Shane would pull in to the drive in a flash-looking Subaru Imprezia or a Mitsubishi Lancer. When he offered us a drive one day I tried to stay cool and pretend I was only vaguely interested, but when he took off at speed I couldn't help but feel the rush. As we tore along towards the neighbouring estates of Fortlawn, Corduff and Hartstown doing hand-break turns and flying over ramps, me and Adam squealed with excitement in the back. What I didn't know then was that these trips were ventures into drug turfs owned by other gangs and the drives were designed as a show of power.

At school I heard the stories of people getting cut up and shot by the Westies, of the addict who owed them a few quid being hung by his ankles from the top of one of the Ballymun towers, of the beatings they were reputed to have doled out at will. But to me Shane Coates was simply Adam's older brother and I thought he was pretty cool. Often he and Stephen would put the two of us on the back of horses and ride down towards the strawberry beds on the northern banks of the River Liffey. It was just like the Wild West and atop the large piebald ponies, I felt like the king of the world.

In reality the Westies were far worse than the rumours going around the classrooms. In years to come I would be under no illusion about the extreme violence they used to assume, in a very short space of time, absolute control over their drug turf. They told dealers to buy their drugs from them, or they wouldn't be alive to sell their lines of coke, wraps of smack and quarters of weed. In fact buying from anyone else led inevitably to a visit to intensive care. They operated a strict no credit policy where even debts as small as £50 would be collected with violence. Hundreds of incidents were reported. One dealer was tortured by having jump leads attached to his nipples. A chronic heroin addict with nine children was burned with cigarettes over a £500 bill while other users were thrown from balconies. They used guns, baseball bats, vice grips and broken bottles.

Of course Ma and Niall eventually heard that I was still knocking around with Adam and that I had been spotted with Coates and Sugg. Niall had been in the pub when someone had mentioned my name and said something about the Westies. I think he nearly died. He told Ma and the two of them waited for me to come in one evening to confront me. "The size of ye," Niall said, looking me up and down. "What do ye think you are at? The fuckin' Westies, if ye don't mind." Ma was quiet. "Joseph, I don't want you getting in trouble. I've told you not to be going over there; now I want you to listen to me." I insisted there was no truth in whatever Niall had been told but he was adamant he was going to nip it in the bud. I was absolutely mortified when he stomped across the road to confront the two of them the first opportunity he got. I could hear him from the house. "He's only a fuckin' child," he told them. I could see Coates and Sugg trying to placate him and promising him that they hadn't asked me to do anything for them, which was absolutely true. "Just leave him alone." I was banned from playing in their house and I often laugh now when I think that to this day, little skinny Niall counts among a tiny few who ever put it up to the Westies.

Just months after they were released from prison the Westies were all of a sudden gone again. It had turned out that the judge released them on the basis they weren't to associate with each other. They had, of course, ignored this and the Gardai were able to prove that they had breached the terms of their release. Even with Shane back in prison I was still banned from hanging around with Adam which I thought was deeply unfair. I remember distinctly I was sulking about that and refusing to go to school. one day when there was a knock on the door and I answered to find a cheery-looking milkman standing there and grinning ear to ear. "Is yer Ma home," he asked. He was wearing a fresh and clean white coat over his jeans and slip on shoes with a bit of a heel on them. He didn't wait for an answer before starting to fire more questions at me. "What are you doing here, should ye not be in school?", quickly followed by, "What ye do wrong den?" I hadn't answered either question when there were another three: "How long are ye living in Ashtown? How many of ye in de family? Where is yer Ma, does she work?" He was friendly and chatty but very pushy and before I knew it he was standing in the kitchen and looking around. He made me feel a little bit uncomfortable but he talked so fast I didn't have much time to dwell on it.

I had seen other kids sitting on the back of the milk floats as they drove around the estates. I knew they earned some pocket money collecting bottles and delivering dockets for the milkman and wondered whether there was a chance of getting a bit of a job myself. So I decided to chance my arm and ask if there was any work going.

"What age are ye? Ye look about 10," he said laughing.

"I'm just gone 12," I said. "I know I'm small but I can run real fast."

The milkman looked me up and down. "Are ye really? I'll find out. I'll ask yer Ma; where is she?" he said cackling with laughter.

"I swear I'm 12. I wouldn't tell ye a lie." I insisted that he could ask anyone he wanted and look at my birth certificate if he had to. I couldn't believe my luck when he told me there was some work and that, in fact, I could start that Thursday.

At the gate the milkman flashed me one last toothy smile. "I'm Brian, by the way," he said. "Brian Kenny. See you on Thursday, don't be late." I literally couldn't wait to tell Ma about my stroke of good fortune landing my first job..

"Ma. I've huge news. I'm after gettin' a job," I told her as she put one foot through the door. She stifled a laugh. "Go on," she said, looking at me quizzically. "On a milk round, Ma. The milkman says I can have a job."

The negotiations went on for some time but in the end it was agreed I could take the work on the basis that I stopped "acting the maggot" about school. I remember that night when Ma settled down on the couch with a cup of tea and a biscuit, she told me that she was happy for me and that it was good something was working out for me. She told me that while I was a messer, I was also a good child and she liked the sound of Brian with his happy smiling face. "It's very important, Joseph, to earn an honest living and not to be relying on the welfare like your Dad. You feel much better about yourself when you work for your money." She warned me that I was to do a good job for Brian and that I was not to be cheeky. Then she threw her arms around me and ruffled my hair. "I just want you to stay out of trouble, Joseph. You have a nose for it. And you're a good boy," she said. But she had no idea how right she was about the trouble.

Joey was just an innocent 11 year old
when he got his first milk round with
Brian Kenny.

CHAPTER 3

Thursday night couldn't come quick enough and I had my outfit picked out: my best Adidas tracksuit with buttons down the side of each leg and matching runners. Ma had bought them for me as "good wear" but as far as I was concerned I had to look my best for my first evening on the milk float. "Ma, I'm wearin' them. I promise I won't get them dirty. I absolutely promise." I think she just gave up after a while. I left them folded and ready on the chair at the bottom of my bed. I sprinted home from school, got dressed and spent the whole afternoon pacing around the house, checking my watch and essentially glued face-first to the front window.

"What time is it? Ma, what time is it?" I must have asked her every 10 minutes until eventually I heard it. The float was a big electric cart emblazoned with the Premier Dairies logo on the front and along the sides. The back was open and filled with milk bottle crates and boxes covered by a thin metal roof. While it was designed to be quiet when it replaced the traditional horses and carts in Dublin in the late 1960s so as not to wake sleeping customers in the early hours of the morning, no engineering could eliminate the rattle of the bottles. And it was that cheery clinking that announced Brian Kenny's arrival at my door shortly before 6pm.

"He's here. I'll see ye," I roared slamming the front door behind me and racing out of the house towards the gate. Brian was in the cab smiling from ear to ear, with a blonde woman who was smoking a cigarette and wearing red lipstick. She gave me a friendly wave. Brian beamed a huge smile and motioned for me to hop on the back which looked much higher up close than it did at a distance. "All aboard," he roared. I took a little run at it, threw my butt up and swung my legs over the edge until I steadied myself. "All right at the back there?" Brian called and I heard him laugh. The float jerked and then hummed forward and I inhaled the moment. The smell hit me immediately. It was a strange mixture of metal, rain and sour milk but it was to become very familiar. The steel floor of the cart felt cold through my clothes and I quickly found out that I had to hang on to one of the poles holding the roof up as we bumped along or I could easily fall off.

Around the corner, not far from my house, the float stopped and other boys got on and nodded to me. "How're ye?" one of them said. I noticed how graceful they were as they swung up like gymnasts beside me. I decided I would study their techniques. One of the boys was nice and started chatting.

CHAPTER 3

"Is dis yer first night?" he asked me and I told him it was. As the crates clattered behind us, he told me the blonde lady with Brian was Rita, his girlfriend, but lots of people thought she was his wife. "They'll show ye the ropes. Just make sure that you keep yer tips in a different pocket to the money for the bills. Don't mix dem up. Put yer money in one of yer pockets with a zip." I liked this boy and hoped I could stick with him for the evening, but when the float pulled in at a big estate in Porterstown, Rita got out and motioned for me to go with her.

The boy I'd been talking to nudged me, raised his eyebrows and made a funny face, giving me two thumbs up as the float drove away. The estate was far posher than where I lived and some of the houses even had electric gates and two or three cars in the drive. Other houses weren't as well kept and had big overgrown gardens and broken gates, but by and large it was, in my mind, very fancy.

Rita smiled and lit up a cigarette. "What age are ye? Brian says yer 12 but ye look about 10. No offence," she smiled.

"No, I am. I promise. Ye can ask me Ma," I said, worried that I was going to be sent home before I'd even started.

"It's all righ'. I believe ye. Small fry!" She laughed and kind of ruffled my hair before she took out a book of little dockets with printed lines on them. She showed me a figure in the bottom right hand corner which she said was our bill and was all I needed to worry about. She told me we were to call on the houses and collect the money for that week's milk deliveries. "Now we've a lot of houses to get through Joey and I'll need ye to pay attention and help me out. Can ye do tha'?" I assured her I could.

Rita unzipped the bum bag wrapped around her waist and for the first time I noticed a little bump and realised that she was pregnant. She took out a handful of coins and notes. "This money is our float and we need to make sure not to fuck it up. I will hang onto it and give you whatever change you need.' As she came to the end of her cigarette she reached into the bum bag and took out a packet of Benson and Hedges. Pulling out a fresh fag she slipped it into her mouth and used the burning butt of the old one to light it. "Do ye want one?" she asked, offering me the packet.

Rita was nice. She wasn't bossy and she laughed when I made jokes. From what I could gather she quite liked me and I quite liked her, which was as good a start as any. I watched her as she walked towards a house with the number 21 painted neatly on a gatepost, flicking her cigarette into a bush as she did. She got to the door, rang the bell and then handed the docket to an elderly gentleman. She turned round to me and playfully stuck her tongue out as the man shuffled back down the hallway before returning with some money. Rita reached into the bag and then handed the man some change. As she walked back out the gate she shouted back that she would see him next week.

"See," she said. "It's easy. You'll be grand, small fry." I wanted to tell her that I wasn't thick and that I would easily be able to cope with what had to be done. It was hardly rocket science but at the same time I didn't want to insult her, so I just let her get on with it and nodded. "I'll do me best, Rita," I said.

I had to watch her do the same thing for the next few doors and each time she told me that the amount at the bottom of the docket was what the people owed. "Most of the time they pay in full but sometimes they don't have enough cash and just pay some of it. When tha' happens I write the amount they have paid on the docket and put me initials after it. I mark them red for paid and blue when money is owed and I put them back in de book," she said. "I'll have to count and check later to make sure it all adds up."

I couldn't wait to get going and eventually she handed me my first docket and watched with amusement as I sprinted off across a green patch towards a large house on the opposite side of the road. "Don't fall on yer face," she called after me, laughing. I might have been small but I was always a very fast runner and was only slightly out of breath when I got as far as the large mahogany door. I pressed my finger on the bell and waited as I heard footsteps approaching along a wooden floor. An elderly man with white hair and a tea towel over his shoulder stood in front of me. "Hiya mister. I'm here for the milk money." I pushed the docket into his hand and gave him a big grin. The man closed over door and I heard shuffling noises before he opened it again and handed me a crisp £10 note. "I'm sorry son that I don't have the right change. I hope that doesn't inconvenience you at all." I told him not to worry and ran back across the grass to Rita who was walking out of another house lighting up a cigarette. I handed her the money and the docket and she counted out £2.60 change. Then I sped back to the customer and he gave me two coins as a tip. "Thank you very much mister, have a very nice evening," I said in the poshest voice I could muster. I couldn't wait to show Rita what I'd got and I took off again across the green and peeled open my fist to show her what was in my hand. I must have looked pretty chuffed with myself because she pulled on her fag and rolled her head back and laughed kind of fondly at me. "You'll be a millionaire before we know it." Then she pinched me on the right cheek.

We worked out our routine fairly quickly. I would be sent to the houses across the green while Rita worked the side she had started on. As the evening wore on the bum bag was filled with wads of money and I was a bit worried we could be robbed. After every few doors Rita would light a Benson and Hedges cigarette and stand and smoke it before she would get going again. She always offered me a fag too. Once or twice I'd take one but I didn't really like the taste in my mouth or the smell of it on my clothes.

I'd keep my hand in my change pocket as I ran from one side of the estate to the other just in case my tips would fall out. As the night wore on, my pocket began to bulge. "I'm making loads of tips Rita," I told her. "I can't believe it. The people are all giving me money."

CHAPTER 3

She laughed. "That's because you are sweating bullets and your cheeks are as red as a tomato. They know you are working hard."

Rita was wrong but I didn't want to correct her. It was actually because I was being extra nice to all the customers. I had quickly learned that the friendlier and more polite I was to the people at the doors, the more likely I would be to get a tip.

"All the 'auld ones like to talk about the weather and the television," I said to her. "I suppose they just like having someone calling. I was invited in a few times but I told them I didn't want to dirty their lovely carpets." We both giggled. As the night wore on I felt rich and free and before I knew it we were done. Although I had been running for three hours like a marathon entrant, I was still full of energy when I heard the jangle of bottles and the electric hum of the float as it pulled up to collect us.

"How did my boy do?" Brian asked as Rita climbed back into the front of the float, a cigarette dangling from her red lips. I was chuffed that he had called me that. "He was a diamond," she said. "The best I have ever worked with and he runs faster than anyone else. He was a brilliant help and did just as he was told." Brian leaned over and kissed her. "I told ye he'd be a good one. I knew the minute I met him." She winked at me and I'm sure my cheeks reddened with pride.

When I got home I turned my pockets out on the kitchen table and told Ma and Niall all about my evening, about the woman who had offered me a glass of water, about the dogs and the cats and the big houses in Porterstown. I must have counted my tips 10 times or more. I sorted the copper from the silver and then mixed it all up again, restacking them in matching rows. Ma boiled the kettle and made me up a fresh ham sandwich. "For the working man," she said as she set it down in front of me at the table.

The following evening I did it all again. I waited by the window until I heard the bottles clinking in their merry dance, I sprinted down the driveway and side-kicked myself up onto the float, breathing in the smell of the sour milk. Me and Rita were again dropped off together at another big estate where I ran like hell for hours while she re-applied her lipstick and smoked on the kerbs. By Friday evening when I was dropped home I was exhausted but thrilled when Brian handed me two 10 pound notes – my wages for the two nights' work. "Ye earned tha', now enjoy it," he said. I was almost speechless. Ma walked down the drive to meet me and Brian leaned out from his cabin with a huge smile on his face and introduced himself. "He was brilliant Mrs O'Callaghan. He can come again," he shouted, flashing a grin and winking before pressing the float into drive.

Inside I upended my pockets for the second time and lined up all the money from the two nights. "13 pounds and 75 pence plus my pay makes up..." I paused. "Loads of money." For dramatic effect I threw the two tenners into the air and let them float back down to the table. Then I picked one up and extended it to Ma. "That's for you Ma. That's for me keep." I must have looked very funny because Ma started to laugh and then stopped herself and looked at me very seriously. "Joseph you keep your money love," she said.

Ma told me years later that she remembers that night so vividly. She says I was always generous, one of the things she loved about me the most. She told me that when I was younger and had my first Communion, I had divided up the money I got and told her to buy herself something nice. I don't remember doing that but she swears it is true. She said that night when I offered her my first wages, she had one of those moments when her heart almost burst.

As the weeks passed I looked forward to Thursday and Friday evenings when me and Rita would be dropped off at the estates and share our work. I was pretty good with the money and soon I found a polite way to tell Rita what change I needed so she didn't have to scribble the sums down and work them out. We'd chat incessantly. She told me she had lived in Ballymun too with her daughter Robyn but like my Ma and Da, Rita had split up with her partner. She said she had worked in a petrol station shop for years and that her own Ma had minded Robyn. "I met Brian when he offered me a lift one day when I was stood at a bus stop with Robyn. It went from there," she said, smiling. I could see she was madly in love with him. She told me that a few years previously she and Brian had bought a house which she called Mitchelstown Cottage, and it sounded lovely. She told me about going out with Robyn and picking blackberries in the fields around the cottage and how Brian's Da, Billy, was doing loads of work for them making wardrobes and fixing things up in Robyn's room. "It'll be finished one of these days and we'll have it lovely. We've a baby on the way now too," she told me, patting her tummy. Sometimes Rita brought Robyn along and I'd mess around with her and make her laugh. She reminded me of my little sister Natalie.

I felt sorry for Rita but I couldn't quite work out why. Most nights she would find a shop to buy a packet of cigarettes and she'd encourage me to get myself a fizzy drink. "Have ye tips yet? Get yerself a bar of chocolate too. It'll keep ye going," she'd say. I kind of knew she would have liked to have bought them for me but Brian was very particular about the money. Sometimes I'd hear her apologising to Brian for had taking £2.50 for a packet of Benson and Hedges and promising to pay him back. I think I must have recognised something in her, something I'd seen in the women of Ballymun, something broken. Sometimes she seemed very vulnerable and she'd panic if she thought the dockets wouldn't add up. "Jesus Christ Joey, there's 20 quid missing," she'd say as the colour would drain from her face. "Check again. I bet it's there," I'd encourage her, knowing that she'd just miscounted. When it came to money she seemed almost afraid of Brian, but from what I could see, he was nice to her when she handed over the takings for the milk.

CHAPTER 3

Sometimes Brian would wave to me to sit up front with him and Rita as we went on our rounds. The other boys were jealous but I didn't care. I loved sitting between the two of them as Brian cracked rude jokes and Rita pretended to be horrified. "Look at the rack on Rita, nearly as nice as your Ma," he'd say. I didn't like him making comments like that but I'd smile anyway. Often Brian would come in when he dropped me home and sit down at the kitchen table for a cup of tea. It was a little uncomfortable. He'd sort of try to flirt with Ma or he'd made lewd comments about my sisters if they left the room, particularly when Rita's baby was due . I laughed along but mostly tried to change the subject so he'd stop.

I had figured out for certain what I was going to do in life. I wanted to be a milkman just like him; in fact apart from the rude remarks I actually wanted to be Brian. My ears pricked up one evening when I overheard him ranting at Rita about one of the boys who worked for him on the rounds. I don't think she was even listening to him. "Jessie is fuckin' gone and I'll tell you something, he will know all about it when I see him. He fuckin' stole from me, Rita. Stole. Can you fuckin' believe it."

He turned around and saw me listening in. "Anyway he is gone now and that is it. Good riddance to bad rubbish." I had no idea why you would risk such a good job for a few bottles of milk but I did hope that Jessie's stupidity might open new opportunities for me. As the school summer holidays approached I knew I'd be free for three months and I'd love nothing better than to spend them with Brian.

At home there was huge excitement after Ma announced that she and Niall had a big surprise. "So we've booked a holiday for everyone. We are going to Gran Canaria and there will be a pool and a beach and as much ice cream and pizzas as we can eat," Ma said. The pair of them loved those big announcements but for the second time I probably didn't react the way they thought I would. I had never been abroad before and while Gran Canaria and the sun and the villa with a pool sounded very exotic, I didn't want to miss work. I reckoned I was onto such a good deal that if I missed even one week on the float someone else would swoop in and take my place.

"Ma, I think I'm going to give it a miss. I've work on and I don't want to let Brian down. I'm sure one of Natalie's friends can go instead of me."

Ma looked hurt and she wasn't having any of it. "You are coming on the holiday Joseph. You are 12 years old and work can wait. Me and Niall have saved very hard to afford this trip and I want the whole family to be together for a little while. It's only one week and I'm sure Brian will keep your place for you," she said.

Reluctantly I told him that I would have to miss the first week of the summer but Ma was right and he assured me that the job would be there for me when I came back. "Rita says we'll never find a young lad that works as hard as you kiddo," he said.

Gran Canaria was exactly like the photographs in the brochures. The sun shone every day and I lay out under it like a salamander until I turned a deep shade of red. I swam and even dug sandcastles on the beach much to the amusement of Ma and Niall. Ma laughed at me, "You're not the big fella now." Like the other young lads on holidays with their parents I suppose I was half man, half child, not really knowing whether I was one or the other. I bought trinkets for Robyn on the market stalls so she could hang them in the new room Billy was making for her at Mitchelstown Cottage and I forked out for two cartons of cigarettes in duty free, one for Brian and one for Rita. "I know they would really appreciate the thought," I told Ma.

There was good news waiting for me when I got back. I could carry on working evenings but, if Ma let me, I could also start doing the morning deliveries with Brian. "I have a spot for you," Brian said. "I'd a bit of trouble with another young lad. He's gone now." I told him I wasn't sure Ma would let me but reckoned if we both worked on her we might get around her. I was right. Ma wasn't convinced.

"I don't want him getting too much of a taste for work, to be honest, Brian. I'm already struggling to keep him in school and I really want him to finish. He's only going into the second year and I know it will be good to keep him busy over the summer, but it's too much." Brian cocked his head to one side and grinned at Ma.

"You don't want him hanging around now, Mrs O'Callaghan, do you? After all trouble is never very far away now, is it?" He motioned his head across the road towards the Coates house. "I'm sure you would think it was much better if he was kept busy but it's up to you Mrs O'Callaghan, up to you."

Ma knew he was referring to the Westies. She told him that she had read in the paper that a Garda had made comments about Shane Coates being "evil" ,saying that he tortured people. "I'll be honest, I don't want him anywhere near that Coates fella or any of the other young lads that seemed to have Blanchardstown overrun," Ma said. Brian nodded in agreement.

"Well Mrs O'Callaghan, I seem to be the solution to your problem and not the cause of a new one. I will keep him out of trouble for you." He grinned from ear to ear and seeing Ma's resolve weaken, I came in for the final blow. "I absolutely promise ye it'll just be for the summer and I'll go back to school in September. I promise ye on me nanny's grave." She grinned a bit. "Don't be saying things like that Joseph. But alright. If you promise."

Afterwards, when Brian was gone, she told me she hoped I would be true to my word. "You seem to like Brian and he seems to be good for you. So stay out of trouble. Now go on with yourself." Brian had become a bit of a father figure for me.

CHAPTER 3

I loved Niall but I'd never quite looked up to him in the same way I had my own Da. Maybe that was simply because I didn't want to let me Da down or think he was being replaced in some way. But Brian was different. I found myself hanging on his every word and while I'd never admit it, I was practising trying to sound and act like him when I was on my own.

The deliveries were to run every night except Saturday, as nobody got fresh milk on Sunday mornings and the milkmen needed a day off. The plan was that I would work 2am to 6am with Brian picking me up at the house and dropping me home. I'd carry on with the collections on Thursday and Friday evenings too. The hours wouldn't have to everyone's taste, but if I wanted to follow my dreams and become a milkman, I'd have to get used to them.

Brian had a large delivery route that took him through the vast housing estates of Fortlawn, Hartstown, Sheepmore and Huntstown, where swathes of social housing were mixed with privately owned properties like ours. Although not high rise, these estates were a bit like Ballymun. They'd been built quickly but without the infrastructure and community services to cope with a population rapidly approaching the 100,000 mark. Like Ballymun, Blanchardstown too was quickly gaining an unwelcome reputation.

Everyone knew about the drug wars at the heart of the regular stabbings and shootings. You'd hear on the streets that Coates and Sugg would be out of jail again within months, which was really going to set the cat amongst the pigeons. I had heard that in the meantime their pals, the Glennon brothers, Mark and Andrew from Hartstown, were making a name as big heroin, cannabis and cocaine wholesalers to smaller dealers. Brian was really interested in it all and questioned me about who was who. "I don't know the Glennons to be honest," I told him. "I knew Coatsie when I hung around with Adam but I don't anymore."

The work was exhausting but I loved it from the moment I started. I would head to bed early or grab a few hours' sleep on the couch but I'd be up for 2am waiting for the chink of the bottles and the electric hum of the float coming down the road. I loved sitting up front in the cab with Brian and enjoying his banter as we drove around the quiet streets. "Look at dem lips on ye," Brian said to me one night. "Big juicy lips. I'll have to call ye Joey The Lips from now on. What ye could do with dem lips." We both laughed but there was something a bit uncomfortable about what he'd said. None the less I was delighted to be given a nickname and anyway it sounded quite cool.

At first I did most of the running: five bottles to one house, two to another. We delivered to factories, traveller-halting sites and even shops. Brian looked after some houses himself while I ran to and from the float grabbing the orders and quietly leaving the bottles on the doorsteps as the customers slept. When he wasn't talking on the phone Brian would entertain

CHAPTER 3

me with stories about his rows with rival milk companies. "I just fuck their stuff in the bins and leave me own," he told me. "It's just a missing bottle here and a missing bottle there. The customers just want a milkman who is reliable, do ye know what I mean?"

He often asked me to lean over a wall and knock over the Avonmore deliveries so it would look like the other milkmen were sloppy with their work. As we drove along the quiet roads, Brian told me that one day I could take over his route. "All dis will be yours, one day The Lips. Ye can have it all. I'm goin' to live in the country when I've enough money. And dat is it. I'll never look back." I could feel myself almost bursting with happiness. There was nothing I wanted more.

In the mornings we would return to the big Premier Dairies depot on the Finglas Road and drop off whatever milk we had over, as well as the empty bottles which would be cleaned and refilled for the next morning. In the dairy yard, the other drivers would call Brian Johnny Handsome.

Sometimes Brian would invite me up to Mitchelstown Cottage after our shift and Rita would cook up a fry of sausages, rashers and eggs with big mugs of tea. She was getting a bit bigger then and I knew she wouldn't be able to continue working for too much longer. I'd roll around the floor and play with Robyn while Brian tinkered around outside. Billy was often there too and I felt really at home with them all at that time.

Night after night I'd be ready on time and I always wore my fastest runners. Ma had long since stopped complaining about me wearing my "good gear" to work as I had been able to buy lots of trainers and tracksuits with my own money. I seriously must have been the best worker any milkman had and Brian was full of compliments. "What would I do without ye, The Lips. You're de fastest I have, the best man on de job." I'd jump from the float, bottles in hand, and be back before I could barely have been missed. I'd time myself and try to break my own records. I could scan the dockets and get the orders correct time and again without even rechecking. I never dropped the milk, never made too much noise in the doorways and never ever complained. For me, sitting up at the front of the milk float felt just like the nights I sat under the stars with me Da. This was happiness for me, the way the world should be. I'd beam from ear to ear as we clattered along and I began to look forward to the fry ups Rita would provide when we were finished.

And then one night everything changed. It happened in an instant, in a flash and without warning. Like the night Ma told me we were leaving Ballymun, nothing would ever be the same again, but this time I couldn't run away. Looking back now, I feel I was a bit stupid not to cop on to what was happening. It did cross my mind as odd, however, that Brian had chosen particular houses to deliver to himself, meaning he had to turn off the float, get out of the driver seat, and then have to get back in and start up the electric engine again. "I'll do dat for ye Brian. You stay where ye are. I don't mind. I can do it," I had offered a few times but he had been almost gruff with me. "I'll do it. Get on with yer work." He wasn't half as fast as me and I assumed that maybe he wanted to stretch his legs or didn't want to put too much on me.

That night we pulled up outside one of these houses in the Sheepmore Estate. I knew one of the blokes that lived in the house. He was a junkie called Paul and he was barred from all the shops in the area because he liked to steal anything that wasn't nailed to the floor. Apart from wondering why Brian did some houses himself, I had also mused once or twice how unusual it was that Paul ordered milk. Like most junkies he was painfully thin with a sunken face, and didn't look to me like a fella who would tuck into a breakfast cereal or down a pint of milk with a cheese sandwich.

Brian turned to me and switched the engine off. I sat looking at him not really knowing what to expect. I couldn't read him. The Brian I knew was gone. He was completely silent and a streetlight shone through the windscreen lighting up his face. I could see that his whole demeanour had changed. The wide cheerful grin and the sparkle in his eyes was gone; instead his face was set in a snarl. "One bottle of milk and put this through the letterbox," he barked at me, his mouth contorted and his eyes wide and menacing.

I looked down at my hand and fingered the package of brown stones. It looked almost like someone had reached down and taken a handful of muck from the ground. I felt a chill rise up my spine and my heart began to pound in my chest. I remember my mouth moved but nothing came out. For an instant I thought it was a joke and that Brian would clap me across the back and roar with laughter. Even if it was a joke I was going to tell him that I didn't find it funny because Brian was scaring me. My breaths became shorter and my head felt heavy. I looked at him but there was no laughing, no back-clapping. This was serious. I got up and swung onto the pavement below. "Make sure you hear it drop and knock the door once. Comprende? Do it fucking right." With that he clenched his fist and gave me an icy glare.

I could feel my legs wobble as I made my way up the drive. The house was unkempt, the garden overgrown and a dim light shone through the sagging curtains in the window. I glanced back at the float, half expecting to see Brian curled over with laughter, but from 10 metres away I could see his eyes were still steely and menacing. "I'm watchin' you, The Lips. Get it fuckin' done." I placed the bottle of milk on the step and knelt down to the letterbox, pushing it open and slowly poking the package through until I heard it thud on the floor below. I got up, knocked the door and dashed back to the float unsure of what I had just done. Brian smiled, slapped me across the back and chirped, "That's my boy," as he placed the float into drive and moved on into the darkness.

Later that night I did it again. And again. Each time I was terrified as I made my way towards the doors with Brian watching me intensely from the float. All the while Brian seemed to slip from one personality to another like a Jekyll and Hyde character. Between these special deliveries he would chat away as if nothing was happening and shower me with compliments about my speed. He told me again and again that I would soon have it all. "Ah yer a great young fella. The best I've had. Ye could be a marathon runner the way you move," he said.

When we finished he cheerily drove into the Premier Dairies depot and threw me a tenner, telling me it was "just a little extra" on top of my wages. The two milkmen called Peter, Peter Joyce and Peter Kiernan, who worked the neighbouring estates in Blanchardstown, were there as usual but for the first time I noticed the trio bunch into a tight group as if they were talking business. They glanced over at me a few times and smiled, making me feel very uncomfortable.

There was something nice about going back to the cottage that morning despite what had happened. Rita and Robyn were there and everything seemed normal and safe again. Brian acted normal too. "Hi love, have ye de breakfast ready? We're fuckin' starving." After we ate he seemed to keep me there longer than usual. I wanted to get home to be on my own so I could think about what had happened. When he finally dropped me back it was late and I barely had time to get some sleep before I was due up again for work. "You done a great job today. I might not even tell your Ma what you did, if you are good. Yer Ma might not be too happy with ye." He cocked his head to the side, held my eyes and smiled. I froze. Smack dealers were scumbags and criminals; had I just become one? "Keep this between us kid if you know what's good for you," Brian said as he beeped his horn and cheerily drove away.

Inside, I tried to process what had happened. While I had been surrounded by drugs all my life, from the junkies on the landings in Ballymun to the vicious smack dealers I heard about in the school yard, I had never actually considered what drugs were. I had never wondered what they looked like or felt like. Lying on my bed I curled and unfurled my fingers over and over again, remembering the tiny stones and the dirty brown colour of the smack. Waves of panic flooded over me as I considered what Ma would say or the look on me Da's face if he knew his son had posted drugs through someone's door. What if I was arrested? What if those junkies died when they took the drugs I had dropped through their letterbox? Would it be my fault if they died?

I tossed and turned and tried to sleep but I couldn't. The chants from my childhood, "Pushers out. Pushers out", replayed over and over in my mind. I had a secret now and it felt like a huge black cloud enveloping me. Just when the palpitations would start I'd hear a voice of reason and wonder whether this was just part of growing up. After all, Brian was good to me, wasn't he? I'd never seen the dark side of him before and I certainly didn't want to see it again but he was okay afterwards, he sort of went back to normal. Maybe I was silly to be worried and this was just what everyone did. I pulled myself up out of bed and went downstairs to make a cup of tea. I'd have to get some sleep because I was in work in a few hours and I was exhausted. But try as I might, I couldn't shift that sinking feeling of dread in the pit of my stomach. Things would never be the same with Brian again, I knew that. I could still see the change in him – that instant, sudden glance of an inner menace, a demon.

The following night the same terrible theatre played out, but this time it wasn't quite so bad. This time when Brian shoved the package into my hand I knew what it would feel like. This time I wasn't so surprised and I knew to get it over and done with quickly and to just get back on the float and act normal. And as the nights went on it began to seem more and more to be just part of a night's work. Brian would chat away and hand me the smack in one hand and a bottle of milk in the other and watch as I delivered them door to door. "Good man. Another satisfied customer there, The Lips," he'd say. Sometimes the junkies would give me a fright when I realised they were standing behind the door waiting for their gear. The first time a bony hand touched mine through the darkness and grabbed the package, I thought I was going to have a heart attack. Myself and Brian roared laughing afterwards and I re-enacted the scene again and again over weeks on end. It seemed to normalise what I was doing.

As we drove along Brian would be constantly on the phone. He was always telling me he was talking to a Garda and they always seemed to be plotting and scheming. He'd make arrangements to leave things for the Gardai in the fields or tell him where he could find stolen goods. He'd regularly threaten to send him to my Ma's house. "What would she do if they found smack in yer bedroom? Would you be in trouble, The Lips? Would yer Ma give ye a smack? Do ye get it? A smack?" I'd feel sick at the mere thought of what he was saying.

Often the Gardai would be driving past in their patrol cars and Brian would flash the lights on the front of the float so they would stop. Then he would get out and chat away with them about football or the weather. I'd sit there in a cold sweat glued to the seat, knowing that we had a cargo of drugs on board and could be arrested at any minute. But Brian seemed to like living on the edge and anyway all the cops clearly knew him well. "That's me boy, The Lips there. He's helping me out. Working with me," he'd tell the cops. "He's a great man for the deliveries." Then he'd go into peals of laughter as my stomach turned somersaults.

Sometimes when he'd drop me home, he'd come into my house telling my Ma that I was a great lad, a great worker. He'd make smart comments and little insinuations and my blood would go cold. "He's brilliant wit de customers, Mrs O'Callaghan. Keeps dem all happy, no matter what dey want," he'd say, turning and winking at me. When he'd come to collect me I'd run out to the gate because I didn't like him being there in my home, and he knew that. When it was just the two of us it was easier to relax because we both knew my secret. But I started to live on my nerves and became even more desperate to please Brian than ever, to keep in with him so as he wouldn't tell on me. I was scared of him but I kind of knew this was only the beginning. There was a darkness to Brian hiding behind the smile and the happy demeanour. and that nearly made it worse because who would believe what he really was?

One night in one of the estates in Blanchardstown, Brian pulled into a road just as another milk truck, a HiAce van with the side door open, passed by. Hanging off the cabin was a young lad around the same age as me. As the two vehicles slowed to pass one another, the boy looked as if he had seen a ghost, jumped from the van and started to run. "The fuckin' little cunt. I'll fuckin' show him," Brian roared as he threw the float up on the pavement. His face was purple with rage as he leaned down to grab a hammer from the footwell before jumping out onto the road. Before I knew what was happening Brian was running after the boy and roaring at him in the darkness. "C'mere you fucker. C'mon an' I'll show ye. C'mon."

Seconds later I heard the first crack as the hammer came down. Then there were screams, blood-curdling shrieks like an animal caught in a trap and howling for its life. I could hear Brian grunting with the effort. "I'll fuckin' show ye. I'll fuckin' show ye." Bang! Bang! came from the darkness as the hammer came down again and again for what seemed like an eternity. Bones snapped while the screams turned to whimpers. I sat frozen in the front seat of the float. I had never been so terrified in my whole life. The driver of the other van did the same, as the smell of blood seemed to fill the air.

Finally there was silence and Brian returned to the float shaking and covered in blood, the dripping hammer in one hand. "That's what happens to ye if ye ever try to rip me off," he hissed, saliva hanging from his mouth, his eyes aflame. He got into the float and drove it down the road and around the corner in silence. When we were far enough away from the carnage he had left behind, he pulled in and got out to examine his hands and his clothes which were drenched in the boy's blood. Shaking, I took a bottle of milk and peeled off the cap. "Here, try to wash yer hands," I almost whispered, offering it to Brian. He was grateful. He poured the milk over himself, scrubbing with one hand as he did. He rubbed his face, across his white overcoat and up and down his arms, as the liquid ran in a pink river to his feet. The rage subsided just as quickly as it had erupted. Slowly Brian began to regain control of his breath and the shaking stopped. Finally he looked up at me and cocked a grin. "Never rip me off kid," he said, as he jumped back into his seat telling me we had work to do. I honestly don't know what frightened me more, the attack or the way he acted as if nothing had happened afterwards. That night we finished every house and every delivery before Brian drove the float all the way back to Mitchelstown Cottage, where he showered and changed his clothes. I had no idea whether Rita even noticed, because she was still in bed when we came in. Once he was clean we drove back to Premier Dairies. The two Peters were waiting and he quipped to them that it had been a "busy night".

I tried my best to keep my legs from shaking. Afterwards we went back to Mitchelstown Cottage where he insisted I ate, despite me thinking I would vomit at every mouthful. "Give him another bit, Rita, he's had a long night," he said. I could hardly look at him. Rita asked if I was okay, and I had to tell her I'd a bit of a stomach bug. "He's had a tough night, our kid. He learned a few things out there tonight." Brian smiled from ear to ear and told me to clear away the plates.

When I eventually got home I ran straight upstairs to my bedroom and crawled up in a ball. I began to shake violently as fear began to take over my body and my mind. I could hear the unnatural and inhumane screams, playing out in my head and the thumps of the hammer crushing bone and tearing through flesh. I wondered whether the boy was dead, and would be found lying in someone's garden in a bloodied mess. I somehow knew it was Jessie – the lad whose job I'd got. Worse of all was the fact that I hadn't gone to help him. I had been so scared, so paralysed with fear that I had actually let a human being get smashed up like that and I had done nothing.

That surely made me culpable. An accessory? It could have been me and it was crystal-clear in my mind that Brian was a total psycho. I kept seeing his face, contorted in rage like some twisted chainsaw-killer covered in blood. It was in my head now and I couldn't seem to get it out.

What was happening to me? As I drifted off to a fitful sleep I saw moving pictures of the doorstep-drops, but as if I was outside my body looking on. I jerked in my sleep as I felt bony hands grabbing my throat. I looked down and saw I was holding the bloodied hammer bathed in flesh. I knew I was dreaming but I couldn't wake myself up or pull myself away from the images floating around in my head. I seemed to sleep then, deeper than I had ever slept before. When I woke up, Niall was gently shaking me. "Joe, Joe, it's time to get up love. Brian will be here soon."

CHAPTER 4

It is hard to find words to describe how quickly my life changed. One minute I thought I was doing a summer job and the next I was trapped in a dark world I had never imagined existed. Even now I blame myself for walking into the lions' den so willingly, but deep down I know that I couldn't possibly have realised what was going on when I started working on those milk rounds. I often wonder why Brian Kenny picked me and what he saw in me that he thought he could take and use. Did he see that I was vulnerable? Or loyal? What if I hadn't run so fast? So many things swirl around in my head at night as I try to make sense of how my childhood was stolen by a predator.

Literally within weeks of that first night when I pushed the smack through the doorway at Sheepmore, I had become completely engulfed by Brian Kenny. He was always there, always at my side, joking, loud, outgoing and gregarious one minute and then whispering and threatening. In the float he'd joke about my lips and make lewd comments. "Oh the boys would love that," he'd say, licking his lips and grabbing my leg. I didn't like it as it made me feel uncomfortable. At home he'd arrange things so I would stay at Mitchelstown Cottage, sometimes calling in to say he was just driving past, sometimes that he didn't want to wake Ma's neighbours or the girls in the early hours or sometimes telling her he'd a few extra bits for me to do up at his house.

"He can stay up with me tonight Mrs O'Callaghan coz we'll get goin' early," he'd say. I couldn't protest because it would have looked weird and I knew he'd hit the roof if I did. I don't know whether he did it on purpose but very quickly Brian started to share every detail of his smack business with me. The more he told me the more I felt stuck to him, as if with very detail he shared, the chains were wrapping tighter and tighter around me. "We've it wrapped up here, The Lips, and we're only gonna get bigger. The real money is in smack. That's where the money is." Then he'd grab my leg so high up that I'd jump.

He must have felt confident from the start that I would be a loyal slave because he talked and talked and told me everything. The two Peters were working with him, he said, and delivering cocaine and heroin under the cover of their own Premier Dairies floats. Together they had an impressive turf throughout Blanchardstown and Ballymun, and stretching far into Santry. Although I found it hard to believe at first, Brian said his Da, Billy, had a role too and it wasn't just fixing wardrobes at Mitchelstown Cottage. He was bagging the deals and preparing everything for delivery at a house they rented in Drumcondra where he'd go during the day. Brian bought his supplies from a gang in Neilstown who he planned to introduce me to and he said he was building a large shed on his land which he planned to use to expand the business. He was hugely ambitious and I was now part of his plans. "You and me, The Lips. We're gonna hit the big time," he'd say.

I was railroaded so fast I hadn't time to draw breath. It was like I had been existing in a parallel universe, some sort of an extra in a bizarre experiment like *The Truman Show*. Before I knew it Brian had convinced Ma that I should stay at Mitchelstown Cottage with him for the rest of the summer as we were working such peculiar hours there was no point in waking everyone in my house. He told her that I could babysit if he and Rita went out and also help him build the shed in my spare time.

"I heard that Coates lad is due out," he told her. "Trouble, that lad." Billy, he told her, would give me a taste of carpentry and building skills which might be useful if I didn't want to finish school. Ma was reluctant, but when she was invited for tea and sandwiches at the Cottage she seemed happier that everything was in order. Of course it was promised that I'd be back to school in September but I think we all knew that scenario was becoming far less likely by the day.

Brian was immensely proud of his compound and loved to tell me all about Mitchelstown Cottage and its history. It was one of the few small homesteads that had survived the development of Finglas' once-rural outskirts, where vast industrial estates meet the sprawl of Dublin Airport and its huge car parking facilities. The little house stood at the edge of Dublin's most northerly border with County Meath, on a three quarter of an acre site. "The people who lived here provided for themselves," he said. "They'd grow fruit and vegetables to feed their family. I'm doing the same ting really. But wit different fruit, eh?"

A winding country road led to the house, and it was surrounded by huge conifer trees and stood at the end of a small pebble stone driveway. It was a really nice property and with the baby on the way there was still lots to be done inside and out.

Brian loved to tell me how ramshackle the place was when he and Rita had first moved in. "It was in shite. Der were nearly rats livin' in it," he said. The house had needed extensive renovations but Billy, a carpenter by trade, had helped out and had been fixing it up room by room ever since.

During the summer of '97, Mitchelstown Cottage was to become for me far more than just a rural hideaway in the heart of an industrial wasteland —it would become the school of life. It was no wonder Brian had wanted me to start staying there as he was desperate for me to learn how to drive. I was so small that I had to use a sofa cushion to sit on, so my feet would reach the pedals. He taught me how to do handbrake turns in the yard and the best way to take corners in order to get the longest view of the road ahead. "Yer a fuckin' natural, The Lips," he'd say, punching the air at my efforts. "And just look at dem Lips. Can ye imagine how much de boys will love dem." I laughed uncomfortably. "I don't know what ye mean." But Brian was too busy laughing out loud at himself. "C'mon The Lips. We all know." And with that he'd get back to telling me how to drive, as if the conversation had never strayed from the gears or the brake pedal. I was a quick learner and I have to admit I loved the feel of the car under me and the surge of power when it took off at speed.

I was schooled in the use of crowbars, lock picks and pliers, and taught the intricacies of using masks and gloves to hide my identity and fingerprints. "Ye have to learn how to rob so we can make money to buy the smack. Den we can make more money when we sell it. Simple mathematics," he'd say. I had no intention of stealing anything but went along with the schooling because I didn't really know how to stop it. Hidden from prying eyes, Brian would stand and watch me as I sped forward and back in Rita's car while learning how to handle the gears. When I eventually took the car onto the open road in the quiet of night, Brian would time me and either wallop me across the back of the head or hug me depending on my performance. "Dat's my boy," he'd say when he was pleased. The two Peters were regular visitors to Mitchelstown Cottage and I quickly realised that I didn't like either. I learned a whole new language. A "Q" was a £20 bag of heroin that was no bigger than a little stud earring, "half an eight" cost £150 and was the size of a small button while an "8" at £250 was the size of a five pence coin. Brian only dealt in £100 bags of coke, nothing smaller.

He told me how heroin was a downer and cocaine an upper and that some of the junkies would mix them together and inject the resulting substance, which they called a snowball, for an extra rush. "The junkies are scumbags but der is one ting for sure, no matter what else, dey need der fix. Dat means money for us," he'd say. He told me he had only intended dealing heroin but the rich businessmen were mad for the coke and he had decided to expand. He said he had no interest in tablets or cannabis because the mark-up was so little but that if we could get the shed up and running and extra money in we would soon hit the big time. "It's smack all the way. Best product in de world."

I was a quick learner, and particularly in how to read Brian's constantly changing moods. I became desperate to please him which would sometimes stave off the blackness that came over him before he lashed out. Always hanging in the air were the memories I had of that night he had beaten young Jessie. Since then he felt no need to hide his fits of temper and his mood swings. It was as if the veil had lifted and he could no longer be bothered to keep up the pretence of being a jolly milkman. He threatened me with screwdrivers and knives and his weapon of choice, a hammer. "You do as yer fuckin' told, ye hear me The Lips," he'd say over and over again. He wasn't nasty all the time but when he was, he was cruel and terrifying.

CHAPTER 4

When he first taunted me about being gay and laughed that he would "break me in", I reluctantly smiled and pretended I thought it was a joke. But I knew it wasn't. "Look at dem lovely Lips. You could do all sorts of tings with dem," he'd moan, while grabbing his crotch. Sometimes he'd grab me by the neck and pull me so close that I could smell his breath. "You'd like that would ye?" he'd say, motioning to unbutton his pants. I'm sure the blood would just drain from my face as he stared at me as if he was waiting for an answer. There was no answer that was right. To anything. When he'd have his fun scaring me, he'd violently throw me aside like a rag doll and walk off laughing.

At the cottage the guard was down between Brian and Rita too. I knew now why I had sensed something familiar in Rita when I first met her. I knew that the black eyes and the aching limbs weren't just because of clumsiness or the effects of pregnancy as she had said – I knew that she was being beaten too. The more time I spent at Mitchelstown Cottage the more she wanted me to stay. We at least had each other and I would regularly step in and take a beating for her because I was worried about the baby or him going for Robyn. I remember a few times begging him to clatter me around the place to save her, or getting in his face as he lifted her against the wall by her neck, her face purple, her eyes bulging. "Just fight me," I'd say. "Come on, give it to me."

Brian wasn't always mean. He could be generous; not so much with money but with compliments. He loved telling me all the things he was going to give me when I got older, like Mitchelstown Cottage and his milk round. "It'll be all yours. You can have it all." When I worked hard, ran fast and did what I was told, he would throw me a handful of tenners and tell me that "we" were all doing great. When I'd go home to visit Ma he would come in with me and sometimes sit for hours until I'd get up and go home with him. If I stayed over with her he'd be on the doorstep first thing to collect me, asking where I had gone and what I had done. "Ye better have kept yer mouth shut, The Lips. Ye know what will happen if you've been shooting yer mouth off." I think Ma was just happy that I wasn't hanging around all day. Blanchardstown had got really bad even over that summer. There were lots of news reports about raging drug wars, about teenagers having guns and not being afraid to use them and pipe bomb attacks and beatings being doled out by the dealers.

Not for one minute did I think of telling Ma what was happening or asking her for help. I have spent years trying to work out why that was, and have come to the conclusion that I didn't tell her because I wanted to save her. I had no doubts about what Brian Kenny was capable of doing. Not a day went by that he wouldn't warn me what would happen if I ever ratted on him. He would regularly make jokes about Ma's house burning down or he would recite the registrations of the girls' cars. "Imagine yer Ma with the flames all around her, screaming for help," he'd say. I had seen his violence with my own eyes on a number of occasions and had been on the receiving end of his temper and his threats. I knew he was well capable of the things he whispered about in my ear.

Going to the Gardai wasn't an option either as Brian seemed to be very friendly with them, particularly the one he claimed he was always on the phone to, telling him what was going on and who was dealing this and who was dealing that. I wasn't stupid; I could see that Brian was a tout, and that meant he had clout within the police. I was totally trapped and I just seemed to accept it without question. I never even considered a way out, I just knew I had to do what I was told if I wanted to survive. I had brought this trouble on myself, I reasoned, because of my stupidity, so it was now my job to keep a lid on things for everyone's sake.

Of course going home to Ma's had become uncomfortable on other levels too. Since I had started the milk rounds, word had spread fast that I was delivering the smack for Brian. I became worried that Ma would find out what was happening. I knew that if she did, she would be straight down to the Gardai and we would all be finished. Every time I went home, I found myself coming to the attention of some junkies who had taken to waving at me and often shouting after me down the road that they needed some gear. On one occasion I had been forced to punch a junkie in the face as I walked along with Ma to the shops one afternoon when he wouldn't shut up about wanting a deal. I remember Ma being shocked. "Joseph that isn't like you to hit anyone. You should be more compassionate to people," she said. I apologised to Ma but lied and told her I thought he had been about to snatch her hand bag. I then wound up as a bit of a hero, which made me feel worse than ever. When I told Brian he was furious. "He's one of me best fuckin' customers. Ye shouldn't have hit me customer. If it happens again maybe he'll put something through yer Ma's window. Do you know what I mean? Somethin' hot."

The solution, he told me, was for me to take some smack home to my Ma's when I was visiting so when the junkies called. I could give them their fix. "Ye might as well make the sale as not," he said, totally matter-of-factly. I was speechless but Brian was behaving as if it was the most normal thing in the world. I did take the smack home and hid it in a John Player Blue cigarette box which I then stuffed in some undergrowth at the side wall of the house. I was in a constant state of anxiety about that and about everything else. While Mitchelstown Cottage could be fraught at times, it seemed an easier place to be at that point than home.

As September approached, the thorny subject about returning to school inevitably came up. Brian was as insistent that it wasn't happening as much as Ma was insistent it was. "She's just tryin' to ruin tings for you. Ye aren't wastin' time at school and ye can tell her dat. Ye work for me now. End of," he'd say.

Meanwhile Ma reminded me of my solemn promise I'd go back to school in September every time she got the chance.

CHAPTER 4

I tried to bury my head in the sand and not think about it. At night I posted smack through the doors of unkempt houses and cocaine through the polished letterboxes in the more up-market estates near Clonee, where BMWs sat in the driveways. I would often feel bad when I delivered the smack, particularly when I saw tiny trikes and plastic toys strewn across the overgrown gardens. One night I peeked through a letterbox and saw a small child sitting watching TV between her unconscious parents. When she saw movement at the door she seemed to know what to do. She walked over, , picked up the bag and went back to shake her Ma awake.

"Wat is tha' stupid look on your stupid fuckin' face," Brian said to me as I got back into the float. "Do ye feel sorry for the scumbag junkies? Is dat fuckin' it? They'd eat ye alive if they got a chance. They are nothin' but dirt."

Brian beat me savagely at any sign of weakness and told me never to be soft on his customers. He'd hold up his screwdriver or his hammer and remind me that he was well capable of using either. I don't believe any other industry is so unfairly balanced against the "customer". "Are ye feelin' sorry for de dirty junkies again," he'd hiss, reaching under his seat and taking out a machete which he always carried in the float. The first time he brought the gun out and laughed as he pointed it at my head, I soiled myself. "Ha, ha, ha, ha. The Lips just shit himself." Brian thought it was so funny that he did it regularly after that. Each time I would clench, wondering whether my time had come. "Hope your Ma doesn't have to bury ye," he'd say, before lowering the nozzle and throwing his head back in peals of laughter.

Cocaine helped my nerves. The first time he gave me some was one Saturday when he took Rita to the pub and left me at home in charge of the house and Robyn with a few cans of beer and a packet of cigarettes. I suppose on an evening like that, I would drift further and further away from reality as I considered my lot. I remember thinking I'd come a long way from Ballymun Towers and convincing myself if I could work harder, Brian would make enough money to move to the country and I could take over his milk round. When they came home Brian up-ended some coke onto the kitchen table and divided it into 15 or 20 lines. He told Rita he loved her and couldn't wait to welcome their new arrival. He hugged me. "You're one of us now The Lips. Part of the family. Let's have a sniff together. You'll be grand wit me." We snorted line after line until dawn broke. That was also the first time Brian gave me Valium, to help me come down off the cocaine. I realised very quickly why all the women in Ballymun loved the Benzos.

Under Billy's tutelage we'd work on the vast shed during the day. Brian had started to regularly drop me up to one of the towers in Ballymun with bags of Qs and tell me to get rid of them. He couldn't let a waking moment go by without trying to make money. He had an insatiable appetite which was only going to get worse.

CHAPTER 4

September came and I made a bit of a thing about moving home and putting on my school uniform but whenever I was at Ma's I was a bag of nerves and it was all a charade anyway. No sooner had I arrived than I was making excuses as to why I'd be staying at Brian's or needing to spend the weekends with him. Brian had decided that we'd pretend for a while that I was going back to school while he tried to persuade Ma to let me give up and go work for him full time. "She'll come around. She probably fancies me anyway," he'd say. He decided I'd go to school for a few full days a week so they wouldn't cop on. On the other days I'd get there for morning rollcall and then he'd collect me at the back before the second bell. Ma wouldn't know any different and I'd be there sometimes in the evenings when she came home. He was always slagging off Ma. "She doesn't want ye to be happy anyway. She doesn't want ye to get on. We're only doing dis for a while and den I'm going to the country and ye can have it all. She just wants ye to be miserable like her."

When he'd collect me at the back of school he'd have everything ready for me: my spare clothes to change into and a few lines of cocaine. From dropping me sporadically at Ballymun, Brian had quickly realised that there was plenty of money to be made in The Towers and he was desperate for a slice of it. They were just as I had remembered them but this time there was no Niamh or Louise coming to look for me. This time I was on my own and I felt smaller than ever as I picked my way along the landings looking for junkies.

At first the junkies reckoned I was easy pickings because I was so small, and they would try to rob me. I quickly learned the laws of the jungle though, knowing that I'd get a worse beating from Brian than from anyone in the flats. I'd quickly decided that I wasn't going to keep either a large amount of smack or money on me at any one time and developed a network of hideouts in the scrublands that surrounded the towers. A rock, an old pallet and other discarded items thrown amid the rubble and wasteland of the flats became my bank. I would secrete my deals of smack and wads of notes there as I worked the landings alone. That meant having to walk up the filthy stairwells which stank of urine and human excrement and then picking my way through the corridors above. I quickly learned which flats were the crack houses and how to announce my arrival by peeking my head around the door and calling out for business. "Anyone lookin'? Anyone here lookin'?" I'd say. I took lines of cocaine before I started to give me more confidence than I might otherwise have had in that situation, but the junkies didn't care.

Some of the flats had been abandoned and probably once belonged to a family like ours with hopes and dreams of a new start. I became used to pushing the doors open, to be greeted by the dark and the stench inside. The voices would come from the blackness and eventually someone would emerge looking half dead and desperate. "Ye, I'm lookin'," they'd groan. Sometimes I saw a familiar face. Sometimes I'd have to remind myself that they were humans. When I'd sell everything I had, I'd ring Brian and tell him to come get me. I got used to the best times to sell and the best times for me to take a break.

The mornings were very lucrative because the junkies were all sick and desperate for their first fix of the day. Some would have spent the night working the streets and selling their bodies to make enough money to pay me for the heroin to get them through the day. The mornings were also easier because by and large they came to me the minute I set foot in the tower. I'd watch them disappear off into flats or onto stairwells where they would shoot up and feel well again for a short while. Some would "goof off" in filthy flats or on a urine-drenched mattress, others would often have sex openly on the landings while others would simply pass out and I'd step over them as I did my rounds.

By midday business would slacken off and Brian would come back to collect me. He'd take me for a bit of lunch topped off with a few more lines of cocaine to revv me up enough to work the evening. "They are dirty bastards, The Lips. The way they live makes me feel sick. Filthy dirty animals," he'd say as he'd hand me another load of gear to flog to them. I got used to their routine. I'd watch them rise from their sex sessions or early afternoon sleeps and see them make their way to the shopping centres or bus stops where they would steal anything to pay for their evening fix. Then they would get back to me with crisp, crumpled and even ripped notes to buy another round of their filth.

I did build up a clientele but there is one thing you can be sure of about with junkies: they are only loyal to their smack. They'd buy from anyone. There were a few who weren't as bad as the ones in the crack dens. One man used to drive out from the city centre in his company car. He'd a job with computers, he told me, but needed a few Qs to get him through the day. "I'm not an addict or anything, it's just the job, it's very stressful," he'd claim. But he was a rarity. The rest were like the walking dead. They'd fall anywhere, sleep anywhere, shit anywhere and only care about anything when they needed their gear.

I'd easily collect about £1,000 a day in Padraig Pearse Tower. On Thursdays and Fridays we'd collect the milk money door to door plus an extra £4,000 in smack money. I handed every penny of it over. I never once thought of short-changing Brian or pocketing any more than the few quid he gave me. It wasn't just the fear of what had happened to Jessie but I just never had any interest in it. I think not being paid meant I never accepted the reality that I had been turned into a drug dealer. For some reason I believed wholeheartedly that there would be a greater good to it all and that it was only temporary. "I just need to make enough money and den I'm gone, out of here, moving to the country. You can have the milk round, you'll be set up," Brian would repeat. Maybe it was a coping mechanism but I believed in my heart and soul that once he had enough money he would start that new life and I could then make an honest wage on the milk round.

I was nervous all the time in Ballymun in case any of Ma or me Da's friends would see me. I'd always have a story ready like I was going over to see me Da or that I was looking for someone in the Towers. I'd never do business out in the open like some of the others did. I'd always go inside the blocks and around the flats. I hated Thursdays and Fridays when I had to collect the money from the junkies as well as the regular customers. Rita had given up working as the baby was due before Christmas, so Brian would keep me with him all evening. "Just tell them to fuckin' give you de money. Smack dem round the place if ye have to," he'd say. "Dey are nothing but dirty filthy scumbags. They are the dirt on yer shoe." He'd repeat it over and over again but to be honest I couldn't help but feel that I was the scumbag myself for heaping pressure on the sick and toothless skeletons that often refused to answer the door to me. "Ye need to pay up now or else Brian will come," I'd say. I'd sometimes knock a few times and then tell Brian nobody was home, but little escaped him and he would insist they were there but just didn't want to pay up. He'd order me to put a brick through their window or to shout through the letterbox that I was coming back to kill them. "Can ye please just pay or he'll come next," I'd try saying to them, but if Brian caught me he'd flip. Then he'd wallop me for sounding like a wimp and not being aggressive enough. It was ridiculous anyway because I still looked like a child and nobody took me seriously.

Sometimes when they really acted up, Brian might order me to set fire to a car in a driveway. If they still refused to pay a debt and something more serious needed to be done, he'd push me aside and take over himself. "Ye want a bit of a taste of me ye filthy fuckin' junkie scum. Maybe next time ye won't try to steal my money." I often thought Brian enjoyed kicking in the doors and brandishing his machetes and terrorising everyone inside. Once he sliced up a junkie in his bed while his terrified partner ran to the neighbours begging to borrow 50 quid. If I'd had it I would have given it to the girl. "I'm sorry. I'm sorry. Just try and give him the money and he'll go," I whispered to her. I was as terrified as she was. He'd threaten them with guns or hammers. And really they were pathetic, totally unable to defend themselves, eaten alive by their sickness and by the very thing I was pushing through their letterboxes. I often thought of me Da and what he would think. The Concerned Parents were well and truly a thing of the past, mired in controversy and probably too afraid of the new generation of pushers like Brian Kenny. And now like me.

Despite all the violence I somehow felt more part of Brian's world than my own – whatever that was anymore. In November Rita went into hospital where she gave birth to a little baby boy named Conor. He was Brian's first born child, but instead of mellowing him, the experience seemed to have the opposite effect. Rita was sick and had to stay in hospital for a long time. He became more and more stressed and anxious to make money. Nothing was ever enough.

Some nights when I sneaked out he'd pick me up at the end of the road. He'd bought me a phone so he could stay in touch and also a bike so I could make my way up to his place if he couldn't collect me. He was all-encompassing. I remember the guilt I felt when I got the bike like it was yesterday. It was because Ma had bought me one for Christmas the previous year, but Brian's bike was far better and I knew Ma would never have been able to afford it. We told her it was to pay me for some work I had done and she didn't mind. "It's lovely Joseph. Really lovely. Well wear, love. And make sure you stay safe on it." Her sincerity only made it worse.

In the darkness Brian tried to teach me other skills that he hoped I would someday use. We'd scope out houses looking for opportunities to steal cars. He'd often bring take me to a halting site to buy an engine for a Mercedes E class or a BMW to match a car he had spotted on his rounds. After much haggling he'd buy the engines for around £600 and then we'd start to properly watch the house where the matching car was parked. He'd tell me how he would steal the car and put the new engine in to produce what was known as a ringer which he reckoned he could sell for around £20,000. "I'll be able to use dat to buy more smack. We'll be rich and I can move to the country," he'd say, then he'd grab my leg and run his tongue along his lips.

In the early hours of the morning he would tell me all about my rights if I was ever caught actually doing anything. I couldn't be touched because I was underage and I didn't have to let the Gardai take my fingerprints. "If ye ever get nicked, ye say nuttin' do you hear me," he would repeat again and again. "Fuckin' nuttin'." I might not have excelled in the classroom but I was probably a straight A student in the school of gangland. "Ye say 'I'm only fucking 10. I want to go home,' do ye hear me?" I corrected him. "I'm 12 and on my next birthday I'll be 13," I said proudly. It was a small thing but to me it was important. I was becoming a man. "12, 13, it doesn't fuckin' matter. What matters is ye say nuttin'."

Despite listening intently to his every instruction, my nerves always got the better of me if he tried to get me to do anything. Sometimes I could actually hear my teeth rattling as he breathed into my ear. "Are ye ready, The Lips? Are ye ready." On a few occasions I would crawl through the window of a house only to lose my nerve and bolt out the front door empty-handed, telling Brian I couldn't find the car keys. "They just weren't there. I looked everywhere," I'd insist. He would then badly beat me, always around the body, and would repeat his taunts about me being gay and needing to be "broken in."

One night when he pushed me through a front living room window into a house in Clonee, I heard noises upstairs. I sank behind the couch and my chest pounded as I heard the dull sound of conversation. I bent down as small as I could when I heard the noise of feet padding across the floor above. My heart thundering in my chest, I followed the footsteps as they came down the stairs. In the glare of the streetlights I could see the outline of a naked man. He walked into the kitchen and then came back through the doors into the sitting room where I was hiding. I held my breath so tight, my face turning red from the effort as I felt the man's body inches from me as he reached to pull the window closed. "I have to do fuckin' everything in this house," I heard him mutter. Just when I was sure I would be caught, I heard him go back upstairs, set the alarm, flush the toilet and settle back in to bed. Up until then I thought that sort of thing only happened in movies, not in real life. Slowly and as quietly as I could I let out the huge breath that I had been holding in for what seemed like an eternity. I stayed there crouched in the silence for about 20 minutes, praying the man would fall asleep. Eventually I tiptoed across the living room and into the hall where I ran like a hare for the front door, not caring what noise I made at that stage.

Outside, Brian was gone. No car was waiting to pick me up. He had either abandoned me or assumed I was going to steal a car. I had no option but to run but I was about 10 kilometres from home.

As I rounded a corner in the estate I eventually saw Brian's car. As I approached, the passenger door swung open and I looked in to see Brian tapping a crowbar across the steering wheel. "Ye took a long time. Where the fuck were ye?" Before I could even answer I felt the first blow come down on my head. "Stop, stop. It wasn't my fault. There was a man," I said, but he wasn't listening to me. It's hard to explain the feel of a crowbar hitting your skull. I suppose it's a bit like one of those cartoons where you sway about with little yellow birds circling your head. That feeling only lasts a second and then heat rushes to the area which you are convinced has been split open. But the head is quite resilient and it takes more than you would expect to split a skull. As the second blow came, I tried to shield myself with my hands and dived for the footwell to get away from the metal. The remaining blows hit my body after that, my back, my shoulders, anywhere he could reach. I was so stiff the next morning I had no idea how I was going to get my legs into a standing position, but I somehow managed to pull myself up. Red and purple marks were everywhere. The lump on my head was huge but it was covered by my hair, and my clothes would hide the rest. I was just like Rita now, so I did what she would do: I brushed myself down and headed for the kitchen to start another day. "Tell yer Ma we got hopped," he growled at me. "If she even asks, interfering auld bitch."

As the year went on I was staying more and more at Mitchelstown Cottage, citing work and babysitting and God knows what else. When I was home I'd tell Ma a load of lies about going into school and managing to work as well. "Yeah I do me homework. Brian helps me wit it," I told her once. "He's good at the maths."

About a month after my birthday I was home one night visiting Ma and went out to meet up with some of my friends. I was enjoying myself so I decided to stay over and I spent the next day, a Sunday, there too. I texted Brian and told him I'd be up early on Monday and asked him to pick me up at our usual spot near the house. "See you then," I typed.

In the early hours of the morning I got up and went out to meet him but there was no sign of him. Brian didn't just not show up when there was work to do and money to be made and I immediately knew something was terribly wrong. I went home to bed but I didn't sleep very well and in the morning I got up and dressed for school. I wondered whether I would see him around the back of the yard in our usual spot but there was no sign of him there either. I tried to ring his mobile but there was no dial tone. It had gone dead. I phoned the house number and could picture the phone ringing away on the kitchen wall but nobody answered that either. When the answering machine kicked in I simply said, "Ring me."

After that I didn't really know what to do. I spent the day in school trying to pretend that everything was normal but when I went home I just couldn't settle so I went out looking for him and I cycled up as far as Mitchelstown Cottage. If I was going to get arrested by the police I wanted to get some story together which would forewarn Ma. The house was locked up and completely abandoned. I knocked and knocked but I knew there was nobody in and oddly the spare key was gone from its usual place under the rock beside the back door. The side gate was closed but I could hear Rita's little dog barking and I went to try and let it out. Brian didn't get on with his nearest neighbours so I couldn't go and knock there and ask them whether they had seen anything. After sitting on a step for a few hours I eventually decided I would have to go home. Ma knew something was wrong. "What's up Joseph? You are like a fella who has left the gas on." she said. I told her more lies: that I was taking a few days off work, that I'd a project to do for school and wanted to get it finished. I didn't even miss a beat. I was getting good at lying.

More important to me was where Brian had gone and what I should do. The best plan I could come up with was to carry on as normal until I heard from him. Four days later I was lying upstairs on my bed beginning to enjoy having a little bit of time to myself when there was a knock on the door. I ran down to answer it expecting to see one of my sister's friends. It was Brian, smiling from ear to ear but with a strange look on his face, one that I hadn't seen before. "Okay kiddo,' he chirped. "We're ready for work tonight. Sorry about the last few days, I just wasn't feeling very well. Ah hi there Mrs O'Callaghan." I glanced around and could see that Ma had walked into the hallway and was peering over my shoulder.

CHAPTER 4

Her brows were knitted. "Oh I see. Joseph said he was doing stuff for school," she said suspiciously. I grabbed a coat off the hook in the hall and walked outside with Brian towards his car. As we did he grabbed me by the elbow and pulled me so close that I could feel the warmth of his breath on my ear. "We're done. We're fucked. We're all going to get jail. Get in."

CHAPTER 5

Brian liked to model himself on a gangster from one his favourite movies. If he was staying in, he would often send me up to the X-Tra vision video store to rent a handful of movies like *Goodfellas*, *Scarface* or *Pulp Fiction*, which he'd watch sometimes all night while he sat on the couch sniffing coke and drinking beer. "Bring out the gimp, The Lips," he'd say, which meant he wanted me to cut him a line of white. He had some of the video box sets himself and watched *The Godfather* trilogy until he knew the lines off by heart. "Friendship is everything. Friendship is more than talent. It's more than the government. It's almost equal of family," he'd quote in a really bad American accent. He loved everything about Tony Montano, Sonny Corleone, Donny Brasco and Robert de Niro's character Paul Vitti from *Analyze This* which never ceased to leave him crying with laughter. I often used to think that when Brian would go into his attack mode, battering a junkie over a small debt with his machete or even holding a gun to my temple, it was like he was stepping into a role that he had practised to perfection in his head. "I'm gonna make him an offer he can't refuse," he'd say as he'd drum a weapon against the palm of his hand. In his everyday world he talked like the movies too and regularly used phrases like "say hello to my little friend" and "kapish". He kinda sounded silly most of the time with his strong Dublin accent but there was no way I'd have laughed. "Bada, Boom. Bada Bing."

Just like many of Brian's heroes, he wasn't very "gangsta" when he actually faced being banged up. In fact I had never seen Brian so rattled in all my life. His hands shook on the steering wheel and he didn't speak at all until we drove way out into the countryside and found a lonely lane. He finally pulled in, turned the ignition off, then slammed his two hands over and over again on the dashboard. "We're fucked. Fucked. Fucked. Fucked." He looked like he hadn't slept a wink and I could see a vein pulsating at the side of his forehead. I stayed quiet, afraid to open my mouth and alert him to my presence. He seemed to be completely in his own world. "Fucked, fucked, fucked," he continued.

Finally he turned to me. "We are all fucked. We're all going to jail," he said. I looked at Brian and shook my head. "I don't understand. I don't understand what you are talkin' about. I know absolutely nothin'. I waited for ye but ye never showed up. I waited and waited and 'den I went back to bed. Wha' happened?" I was perplexed, but Brian stayed quiet so I continued, "I waited for you at the back of the school. I went up to Mitchelstown Cottage but der was nobody there. I tried to carry on as normal but nobody came. Nobody came near me."

Brian perked up a little bit. "No Gardai? No Gardai came for you? They mustn't know about you, The Lips." That seemed to give him a small amount of relief but he was still like a coiled spring. "I hope you didn't rat! Did ye fuckin' rat? Did ye?" He had me by the throat as his eyes bulged in his head and the vein over his right eye pulsated. I shook my head vigorously. "No, no, course not," I managed to whisper. He let go and started hammering on the steering wheel again.

Over the next few hours he told me everything. "I was arrested. The two Peters were arrested and even me Da was arrested. They came to Mitchelstown Cottage; Rita is freaked out. They were watching me, watching us." Brian went on to tell me that Billy had been lifted at the stash house in Drumcondra where he cut up and bagged the deals. When the Gardai arrived at Mitchelstown Cottage with their warrants, Rita had bundled up Robyn and baby Conor and gone to her Ma's. They'd been watching him, he said, for weeks. "Watching Drumcondra, watching Peter, watching Mitchelstown, watching us all." The cops had literally caught them with their hands on the smack. They'd all been separated in custody. "The only thing I know is that nobody said nuttin'. The one I was worried about was you. I was worried ye'd have ratted me out." I assured Brian that there was no way I would have opened my mouth had I been lifted by the cops but nobody had as much as come to my door. "At least tha', The Lips. At least tha'." But for Brian the glass was definitely half empty. "This is a fuckin' disaster. I'll never be able to move to the country now. You won't get me milk round. I'll be lucky if I can keep Mitchelstown Cottage."

Brian seemed almost vulnerable and I found myself trying to comfort him and telling him that it couldn't be that bad. He was acting almost like a child and he even looked smaller than usual bent over in the car. The cops had told him that they knew all about his operation. He said they knew how he'd using mobile phones to take orders for smack and coke and the floats as cover to deliver the drugs. The only saving grace was they were nearing the end of the load from Neilstown that morning when the cops had burst in. Most of it had already been sold so there wasn't a huge amount quantity-wise to worry about. Still, they knew exactly what he was doing and he'd been under surveillance for months. He said he just couldn't go to jail, he wouldn't be able to do time. "Well they might have told ye they know everything but they don't know about me," I said. "So they don't know everything. They're only winding ye up."

Brian's eyes flickered with recognition. "Maybe they don't know everything," he agreed. "Maybe they are havin' me on." He started to formulate a plan, saying that if he could help the cops out, maybe they would help him. I'm gonna make a fuckin' plan. That's what I'm gonna do. I'm gonna make a fuckin' plan." Brian turned to me with that familiar menacing look in his eyes. "The Lips, you keep your mouth fuckin' shut if they come near you, ye hear me. Fuckin' shut. I don't want you fuckin' everything up."

I told him that I knew exactly what to do. "I won't say nothing. I'll give them a bit of lip and I'll tell them my age," I said. "I'm only just turned 13, mister. I want me Mammy," I said in a sing-song tone. For the first time since we had pulled into the roadside, the mood lightened a bit and Brian laughed. "You're a good lad, The Lips. I trust ye with me life." Despite the violence and all the other things Brian had done to me, it was moments like that which I lived for. Being told I was a "good lad" was all I wanted from Brian. I would have moved mountains for him to be told that,.

After a few hours in the car, Brian had calmed down a bit and his defeatism was beginning to dissipate. The fight was back in him and you could almost see the cogs in his brain beginning to work. He was absolutely certain. The smack was going to stop and we would get ourselves back on the milk round and stay clean until the court case. I could feel relief flooding my body. I didn't care if I had to work every hour God sent to keep Brian on the straight and narrow. It was a godsend that I was never again going to have to push smack' through a letterbox or threaten some junkie for 20 quid. I simply couldn't have asked for a better result and I was secretly delighted that Brian had got caught. It meant a new beginning for us, a fresh start. "I'll work it out. I'll give them everything they want," he said. At that moment the world seemed right again. It was almost as though the past year had been a bad dream. But as I have learned, there are no fairy tale endings or movie plot twists. Hope as you might, the only person you can ever change is yourself.

The new regime began immediately. We were only delivering milk from the float. I was thrilled and I vowed to myself that I would do everything I could to show Brian that he didn't need the smack, that he already had enough. But Brian and I weren't only a lifetime apart in age; we also had very different ideas of right and wrong. For him, "going straight" didn't mean earning an honest living delivering bottles of milk. Instead it meant working as a tout, tipping off the Gardai as to where they could find weapons, stolen cars or goods. "It might just be enough The Lips, to keep me out of the big house. I can't do jail, The Lips. I just can't do it," he'd say. Along with a guilty plea, Brian hoped that his "help" with Garda operations would get him a suspended sentence. Of course there were no guarantees; the judge would ultimately decide his fate and Brian had no influence on the judiciary'. "I've only one option and this is it. I've a new lad and I'm gonna give him everything he wants. Look and learn, The Lips. Look and learn."

At this point we had finished building the shed at the back of Mitchelstown Cottage, complete with a shining new metal shutter to hide whatever was inside from any prying eyes. Brian had invested in a Toyota Dyna van and was constantly moving stuff around. In the grounds of such an isolated house, the shed was the perfect HQ for Brian's new venture and his mission to stay out of jail. "We are gonna make the fuckin' news, The Lips. We're gonna give dem wat they want. We are gonna hand dem it all. Watch me play dis fiddle," Brian said.

Initially he was concerned that he was still being watched by the Gardai. He had become so paranoid that he would sometimes drive in circles on roundabouts to make sure he wasn't being followed or just pull in randomly by the roadside to let any cars behind us pass him by. He'd get all riled up and I could sense the paranoia and stress engulfing him before he would grab the back of my head and bounce it off the float's dashboard. I tried really hard to avoid his ire but it was impossible. He attacked me back at the house all the time too. He seemed to get some sort of relief from battering me. He would go on and on and on about the court case. Rita also seemed to be getting a lot of unwarranted attention from him, particularly because Conor was only a tiny baby.

After a few weeks of circling roundabouts, it was pretty obvious that we weren't being followed and it was time to get down to business. I had new lessons to learn. What the Gardai of course didn't know was that the "newly reformed" Brian, who was helping them out so much, had intimate knowledge of anything he was tipping them off about. He attacked his new project with the same gusto and almost the same ambition as he had the last. Once he got going, not a moment would pass without some kind of work being done. Presumably his handler didn't realise that when he told him about the location of a stolen car in a field in north County Dublin or a loaded gun discovered in a garden - it was actually Brian who had stolen them and placed them there in the first place.

I didn't realise how much politics played its part at the time. Back then, gangland was ruled by a handful of key players, but the Gardai were under huge pressure to tackle crime and to get results. If they found a firearm, it would make the news and make it look like they were doing a great job. It didn't really matter to the public how they found it as long as they were out there doing their job and tackling the gangs.

The biggest player of the time was Martin Marlo Hyland who was in control in Finglas. He worked with the Bradley brothers, Wayne and Fatpuss, and had a mob under him supplying the whole area. My old neighbours Shane Coates and his pal Stephen Sugg, along with the Glennon brothers, Mark and Andrew, were in control of Blanchardstown. In Clondalkin there was the Hinchon mob and a few other gangs fighting for the turf, including one run by a young lad called Simon Doyle. The other big players were Dee Dee O'Driscoll in Ballyfermot and the likes of Brian Rattigan and Freddie Thompson, who were beginning to fight over their turf in Crumlin and Drimnagh. "I've no fuckin' interest in southsiders," Brian would say, whenever any gun crime was reported on the other side of the River Liffey.

Dublin was sliced up by the gangs and each of them was structured in a similar way. All along I suppose Brian had wanted to become one of the big boys and I believe he was well on his way when he was stopped in his tracks. In the Finglas and Ballymun areas there was a young group who were known as the Filthy Fifty, and while I don't think there were quite 50 of them, their numbers were certainly in double figures. They were young lads, a bit older than me, in their late teens and early 20s. They had a reputation of being absolute lunatics and were used by the bigger criminals to do jobs like getaway drivers, robberies and drug deals. The best known fellas in that group were a guy called John Daly who was about five years older than me and a trigger man (the one who ties up any loose ends); Anto Spratt, an expert on big armed robberies, and Deccie Curran, who was an enforcer-type. Collie Owens and Eamon Dunne were also knocking around that group but they were working more for Marlo Hyland than anyone else. Then there was a fella called Paul Farmer Martin, who was a bit older than the others but had a reputation as a bully. They were all pretty violent and you would certainly be keeping your distance from them. Brian was kind of obsessed with them all. He idolised Marlo Hyland and spoke about him as if he was a god.

I seemed to be going to school less and less and spending more and more nights away from home. I certainly don't

CHAPTER 5

remember finishing my second year. Within such a short space of time life had become completely chaotic and unrecognisable from the way it should have been. Brian's obsession about staying out of jail seemed to be all-encompassing for him and therefore also for me. He'd sometimes pace the ground talking to himself and work himself up into a huge rage about it. He was so unpredictable. I tried to please him, hoping to improve his mood, particularly for Rita and Robyn's sakes. Brian knew there was absolutely no way the charges were going to be dropped for something as serious as a heroin bust. Smack had such a toxic reputation at that stage that the Director of Public Prosecutions was never going to change their mind, particularly because Brian had been using a milk round to deliver it.

No doubt Premier Dairies had heard the rumours about Brian and he knew he'd lose his job the minute he went to court and the case became public. I In the meantime he was using the round for surveillance. At night we would deliver the milk and he would work out what he could steal to hand back.

He was constantly angry and on edge. One morning we were delivering milk off the Huntstown Road when Brian parked the van on an area we called the "fat path." There was hoarding nearby where they were building a new estate and after we delivered milk to a few homes, Brian got out of the van to go to the toilet on the path. When he finished he got back into the van and I noticed he hadn't zipped up his trousers. "You lookin' at me?" he asked, his face red and bulging. "No, I wasn't," I said. "Do ye like what ye see, The Lips?" he taunted, grabbing my head and forcing my face down onto his penis. It happened so fast I hardly knew what was going on. I gagged and gasped for breath while he rubbed the back of my head and pushed me forward and back until he was finished. I was completely stunned and disgusted with the taste in my mouth, but he just carried on as if nothing had happened, pulled up his jeans and zipped them up. He was still fixing himself when he started talking. "The Lips, ye know ye are like a son to me and I'm only preparing ye for when ye get older because ye know ye are gonna be gay. Now I don't want ye to tell anyone that I am doin' that for ye because ye will get me into trouble, now do ye hear me? Do ye? You're not to tell anyone what I'm doin' for ye because they won't get it that ye are like a son to me."

I looked out the window at nothing in particular and noticed it was still pitch dark even though it must have been nearly 6am. Beside me he kept talking. "Ye know that I'm only trying to look after ye. I'm tryin' to protect ye. That's why I gave ye the job and I'm trying to keep ye out of trouble. Do ye hear me? Now I want ye to promise me that ye will come back to work. You will, won't ye? You will come back and ye will say nuttin'." He went on and on while we finished the round and he eventually pulled up on the pavement outside my house. "Now I want ye to go in and get ready for school and I will see ye tonight for work. Do ye hear me? You are like a son to me but ye can tell nobody or ye will get me in trouble." He took my hand and looked straight into my face. "Ye know ye are like a son to me, just like a son." I nodded. "I'll say nuttin'." And then I slipped out of the van and made my way into the house. In school I wondered exactly what had happened. I didn't really understand and I certainly didn't think it was supposed to happen with a man.

That night I was apprehensive when I got up at 3am to wait for Brian. I didn't know how he would be and whether he would be angry all over again. The minute I hopped into the van he turned on me. "Did ye tell anyone anything?" he demanded. I told him I hadn't. "Did ye mention anything in school?" I moved my head from side to side. And then it was over and we worked away as normal and nothing happened. I was relieved and I put the experience down to a one-off, something to be forgotten about and never mentioned again.

But a week and a half later the same nightmare played out, this time in a lane by a field overlooking Mitchelstown Cottage. This time Brian was more confident. He moved his seat back, opened his trousers and said, "Same as last time, The Lips." He pushed my head down and when he was finished he got out of the van to fix himself before opening the gate and driving back out into the night where we finished our round. He never spoke about it but just carried on working like everything was normal. And suddenly, like every other line that had been crossed, forcing me to give him oral sex became as ordinary with Brian as delivering a bottle of milk. Every few nights he would pull in to a quiet roadside and force my head down to his lap. I'd close my eyes and will it to be over quickly, disgusted by the smell and the sweat and the taste. Sometimes he would tell me he was doing it for me to prepare me for when I would be gay. Other times he would fix himself up and make a lewd remark about Rita or some girl I knew. He very quickly stopped warning me not to tell anybody; he just knew I wouldn't. I was too afraid and he could sense that from me.

When we had done the deliveries, he'd stalk the industrial estates watching the factories and sizing up any opportunities. In Ballycoolin he stole a truck full of drink and drove it straight to a field in Finglas. "Are ye fuckin' sure about dis?" I asked Brian as we ran through the field towards a getaway car he'd parked up some hours previously. "I'm sure. I'm fuckin' sure." He didn't even take a bottle for his troubles before phoning his handler and telling him where to find the truck. I don't know exactly what Brian said, probably just that he had heard there had been a robbery, something had gone wrong and the truck had been abandoned. "It will look good for the pigs. Dey want to look good. It's as simple as dat," Brian said.

Every so often he would give me a lesson. I could have been doing my masters the way he handled it so forensically. "Dey don't just want the truck, The Lips, dey don't want it empty, dey want it full. Dey want guns to make it look like dey are workin'. Dey want ammo so dey can say dey saved a life. It's not fuckin' Mensa. Do ye know what I mean?"

By the time the robbing started in earnest, I was doing about a oner of cocaine over the course of the day and I had yet to turn 14 years old. That would do me about 20 or 25 lines. If I stayed overnight at Mitchelstown Cottage he would come in to me in the morning, hand me a pile of white powder and line it up for me. He'd put a bowl of cornflakes down beside it. He'd take the same himself but he was clever and more practical with the way he used the coke. "Whatever ye do, don't be taken too much or yer useless," he'd say. "Ye just want enuf to get the adrenalin goin'." Whatever the science, was it certainly gave me more courage than I would have had otherwise. Whether we were going out for the day or the night we'd always take it with us. If he was planning a job we'd take it beforehand. He seemed to have amassed a collection of vehicles in the shed: trucks, vans and stolen cars, and he would use what he needed depending on the job. He often took me with him but I was still only an apprentice and I had no idea how he even cooked up some of the scams.

He planned to rob a jewellery store in Finglas and pull a truck across the window so nobody could see him from the road. By and large I'd be the one who was thrown in first and would hand whatever it was we were robbing out to Brian while the alarms were screaming in my ears and the cocaine was surging through my blood. There is no way I would have had the nerve to do any of it without the sniff. He knew that full well, so he kept me topped up all the time. Life seemed to be a series of scenes, a haze of flashing lights and wailing alarms. Sometimes Brian kept his loot for himself but he was largely obsessed with handing his spoils over to the cops, who still had no idea he was doing the jobs himself. "The Lips, I'm gonna get off this rap, you watch me do it. Look and learn kiddo. Do ye hear me? Look and learn."

Brian stole everything that wasn't nailed down: Mercedes, BMWs, Audis. He left them in fields, in car parks and even beside Dolly Heffernan's pub which was right by his house, when he was too lazy to go any further. He got hold of trucks full of chickens and cigarettes. In the industrial estates he'd cut the locks off the doors and then replace them with his own, setting the alarms off as he did. Then he'd hide in the darkness and wait for the security guards to arrive. They'd look around, see the locks intact and ring in that it had been a false alarm and they should be shut down until the morning. Of course they'd then go back to their huts, allowing Brian to use his own keys to break in. He was a master. Back then alarms were wired down through the shores so he could clip the lines and then pop the windows. Brian put me through any gap he could. He would have sent me down a rat hole if he could.

Once when we were out on our nightly tours we stopped off at a garage to buy some diesel and Brian noticed that a side window into the offices behind was open. He watched for a while and then took me around the back of the building where he decided he would lower me inside by the ankles. I was terrified. I had no idea what I was going to do but I needn't have worried. As I made my way head first through the tiny window, I realised that I was in fact climbing into a loo and the most likely reason that the window was open was because a large foreign man was sitting on the toilet having a shit while reading a newspaper. I started to shout as I realised I was being lowered down on top of him. Brian tried to pull me out and the fella on the pot tried to pull me in. Legs and arms flailed and punches flew until eventually Brian won the battle and dragged me back to the van.

He stole a large, brand new caravan from a garden one night and towed it all the way to Drogheda, leaving it on a lane there. Brian reckoned it was a good one to give back to the cops. He was always telling me I was lucky and that he was just looking after me and securing my future. When he was happy he'd praise me. "Ye know ye are just like me son," he'd say. He'd then rage at how stupid and small and frightened I was. "Ye are just like a fuckin' mouse, The Lips. Ye need to toughen up and speak up. I can hardly hear ye." At the travellers' halting sites around northern County Dublin, Brian would leave me outside and go in on his own. He hated spending money but he told me he had to give up a few firearms to the cops. Eventually a deal would be struck for some sort of a shotgun or a Glock. He'd probably pay about £500 or £600 for it before we'd head off and he'd hide it somewhere in a field or in a garden. I'd then hear him on the phone telling them he'd heard a gun had been hidden there. When he'd finish the call he'd lick his finger and run it through the air in front of his face as if he was ticking off another chore.

Ma was still begging me to go back to school or at least to stay on until my Intermediate Certificate exams But I knew there was no way I would be going into any exam hall. "I'm not goin' back there. I hate it Ma," I'd roar at her. "You're just tryin' to ruin my life. I've a good job and I like it. Why are ye trying to ruin everything for me?" I knew I sounded like Brian but I just couldn't help it. I had so many secrets now; all the lies I had told had completely isolated me from the one person who would never give up on me. . I remember calling her a snob and everything and accusing her of looking down her nose at an honest job like mine. I had some neck really but I was desperate to keep up appearances. To keep her happy I eventually promised I would go on an early school-leavers' course

In the confines of Mitchelstown Cottage Brian was an absolute savage. His violence knew no bounds and he was constantly brutalising Rita and me. Sometimes he'd lock us out of the house, sometimes he'd lock us in. He'd smash up the furniture, mainly to use as weapons on us. I did what I could for Rita because I felt sorry for her but sometimes he would go for her in her bedroom at night. I'd see the results in the morning. I knew Robyn hated him but for some reason I felt kind of sorry for him which made me even more confused. Despite what was happening in the secrecy of the van when he would unzip his trousers, despite the violence he was doling out to all of us, I still somehow liked him and that made me feel like I was the one that had the issues.

When I look back now, I can see how completely screwed up all that was. I was a young teenager, fed on a diet of cocaine and sent out to rob and deliver drugs by a 30-year-old man. And I was being beaten and raped. I was terrified of him and yet I loved him. It used to fill me with pride when people would ask him if I was his son. "He's not me son, but he is like a son," he'd say and I'd feel like I had made it in life. And I really believed that he was trying to do his best for me and for Rita and the kids, that he was trying to make enough money to move to the country and that he was going to give me Mitchelstown Cottage and set me up with some sort of a business. What I wouldn't give for a chance to go back there, to lead the child Joey away to safety . But back then no one was around to do that, to convince me that things weren't right. It would take me years to realise how Brian had tried to turn me against Ma. He must have noticed the closeness of the bond between us and realised she represented the only threat to his power and authority. "She's a stupid cunt, The Lips. She is just trying to fuck up your life. She doesn't want ye to be happy. She's a miserable auld bitch," he'd repeat over and again. I became even more secretive with Ma, way more so that I ever thought I would be capable of. I told her nothing except lies about what I was doing.

The court date finally arrived and I remember the nerves and the stress in the days beforehand. Brian had been working flat out, telling me he was giving the cops two or four cars at a time, ride-on mowers, anything he could get his hands on. I certainly saw some of the stuff in the shed. People were calling Brian a rat because he was touting on other people but he didn't care. He just needed to save his own skin. Since I had turned 14 I had started to stay at Mitchelstown more and more. It seemed easier and less hassle. Even when I would get back to Ma's, Brian came to fetch me to make sure I wasn't spending too much time with her. He was paranoid about who I was talking to and what I would be saying to them.

We all got up on the morning of the court case and the usual suspects lined up in the house: the two Peters, Billy and Brian. There was another guy there that morning who we used to call Auld Fella John. I never asked why he was there but I do wonder what he was doing there that morning. Auld Fella John visited Mitchelstown Cottage about once a month. He was an elderly man and he would just collect or deliver the bags of money. He was a nice polite man. He had big hands despite being tiny like me and he had a huge nose. A small wisp of white hair sat on the top of his head. He drove a bust-up old van but Brian had once told me that he owned lots of houses in Dublin. I had never really any idea what he did with the money but I knew that Brian trusted him and when we were selling the smack he would collect the money and mark it in a ledger. Brian would laugh when he'd see him pulling up the drive and tell me that the "laundry van" was coming.

They all looked kind of funny dressed in suits, particularly Peter Joyce who was overweight and "an ugly fucker" as Brian used to call him. He looked as if he had his Communion suit on and his shoulders were pulled so far back in his jacket that he could barely move. It felt like a wake and I just kept quiet and stood around with them. When they were about to go, Brian called me outside to the conservatory where we could have a chat out of earshot. "You're the man of the house now, The Lips," he said. He was almost on the verge of tears. "You have to look after Rita and the kids. You need to clean the yard and take care of the shed. Do ye hear me?"

I didn't really know what to say. I was thinking how the hell was I going to look after a house and a family I asked him what I was supposed to do for money. "You know what you have to do. You're old enough now, The Lips. Just don't get caught." I didn't want them to go, but when I was left there alone, I looked around and the house seemed like a big mansion to me. There were five bedrooms and the conservatory and the front yard and the shed and then there were the kids and Rita. No wonder he used to get so stressed out, I thought. It stressed me out just thinking about it. I paced the floors as I waited for news. I walked all around the house looking at all that would need to be done. I went out to the yard, looked over the shed and then went back inside. I found cracks in the walls I never knew were there. I noticed the state of the paintwork for the first time. How the hell would I be able to look after all that for him? And what if he got 10 years or something?

Then I began to worry about the other criminals we often talked about who would see how vulnerable I was. Without Brian there I wouldn't have a hope against them. They could take the lot. Brian could get out of jail to find there wasn't a stick of furniture left and he would see me as a total failure. The clock ticked and the minutes turned to hours and there was still no news. I tried to relax, to watch the television but I couldn't. I checked my phone over and over again but nobody rang, nobody texted. I knew not to ring Brian or Rita but I willed them to ring me. I veered from no news being good news to no news being bad news. I couldn't make up my mind.

At about 7pm I heard the cars pull up the drive and I braced myself. I must have looked like a Labrador puppy when Brian walked in the door and opened his arms to give me a hug. I was never so thrilled, so relieved in all my life. I was so glad to have him home. The party went on into the early hours. We snorted lines of cocaine and threw back cans of Dutch Gold and anything else we could find. Brian played the clown and we all laughed at him. He was even nice to Rita and must have told he her loved her a million times. "The Lips! We're back in the game. Bada Boom. Bada Bing."

THE IRISH TIMES

Milkmen delivered heroin on rounds

Three milkmen who used mobile phones to take orders and delivered heroin on their rounds for a major Dublin drug gang have been given five-year suspended sentences. A carpenter who prepared the drugs was also given the same sentence.

Garda Christopher Elliott said the milkmen were recruited by the gang after their businesses fell into financial difficulties.

Judge Elizabeth Dunne at Dublin Circuit Criminal Court described them as "a very unusual group" to come before the courts on a drug supply charge.

Peter Joyce (27), of Abbotstown Drive, Finglas; William Kenny (50), of Collins Avenue, Whitehall; Brian Kenny (30), of Mitchelstown Cottage, Kilshane Cross, Finglas; and Peter Kiernan (42), of The Court, High Park, Drumcondra, pleaded guilty to possession of heroin with intent to supply at High Park, Drumcondra, on February 12, 1998.

CHAPTER 6

He looked every inch the Godfather. Martin Marlo Hyland might have been dressed like the rest of us in a pair of jeans, a North Face jacket and brand new white runners but there was no mistaking him for anyone else as he sat at a table in a back bar of the Cappagh House pub in Finglas. Marlo was a big brute of a fella but it wasn't just his bulk that made you realise who you were in front of; it was as if his aura filled the room too and everyone waited for him to talk. Brian approached the table and I remained a half step behind but still firmly at his righthand side. We stopped short of taking a seat and stood like two soldiers until Marlo addressed us. His eyes rested on me and slowly he looked me up and down with a coldness that sent a shiver up my spine. "I don't talk in front of young fellas." I shifted my weight from foot to foot and wished I could disappear.

For Brian this was the biggest moment of his criminal career. His reputation for robbing had been steadily growing. He had spread the word in underworld circles that he had a

CHAPTER 6

storage shed for stolen goods, drugs, cars and guns at the back of Mitchelstown Cottage. And of course he had me, looking every inch like Oliver Twist beside him. For weeks he had raced up and down through Finglas clocking 180kph past the home of the Bradley brothers: Alan Fatpuss and Wayne. More often than not we were being chased by cop cars – largely because Brian had phoned them anonymously to say there was a driver armed with a gun in the area. It served as boot camp training for me, a crash course in how to outrun and outsmart the Gardai. And as a double whammy, it showed the Bradleys what Brian had to offer.

The Bradleys lived in their Ma's house on the Cappagh Road. They both looked like absolute meat-heads but Alan definitely had more brains than Wayne. They had matching sapphire-blue Subaru Impreza cars with blacked out windows and gold hubcaps which they parked nose to nose across the driveway. They spent most of their time in the garden leaning over the walls and watching who and what was going by. Like their boss Marlo, they knew all about the power of fear and how to maintain their reputation amongst rival drug gangs.

After Brian had escaped jail on the smack charges, he had become more confident and ambitious than ever. He had lost his Premier Dairies contract but immediately set up a "business" collecting pallets at night: just another cover up for what was really going on. The robbing became 10 times worse when Brian was doing it for himself. He was stealing absolutely anything you could think of: construction machinery, cars, vans filled with goods, trucks, you name it. He even nicked a boat one night from the garden of a home outside Dublin and brought it back to the shed at Mitchelstown Cottage. He then went back to the same house to pick up the two jet skis that were parked up alongside it. Brian was so happy with the boat he decided he'd keep it for himself. He got me to paint it to try to disguise it before bringing it up the north east coast where he was planning to retire. It was for "family days", he told me, and one afternoon we even sat on it and had a picnic. Brian had also got hold of a police scanner and was using it back at the Cottage to monitor where the Gardai were and what they were doing. Sometimes he'd go off robbing with other people and leave me at home to manage the scanner. I was supposed to leave the volume on full and listen in to what was happening. I remember a few times when he had given me or Rita a particularly bad beating, I'd turn it off when he went out and hope to God that he'd get caught. Then I'd hear the car coming up the drive and I'd turn it back up full blast.

Brian was desperate to go bigger league and when it came to robberies, there was no one with a bigger reputation than Marlo Hyland. Marlo ran a band of armed robbers, mainly made up of the Filthy Fifty, who were ripping off ATM machines, banks, post offices and even grabbing cash from pubs and bookies. Marlo never got his hands dirty with any of the actual robberies but he was very much the main man.

CHAPTER 6

The profits were pumped straight back into his drug business, allowing him to control the wholesale supply of heroin, cannabis and coke across his turf. At his right and left sides were the Bradley brothers.

Brian knew that Wayne Bradley had a reputation of being good for little more than spotting on jobs, and that Fatpuss was in the market for a proper sidekick. He reckoned he had exactly what it took to get the job. While they were up for anything, the likes of John Daly and Deccie Curran had a reputation for being a bit too hot-headed on jobs and were liable to start shooting at anything – which was sure to bring a whole lot of heat down on everyone. Fatpuss was looking for someone who could keep calm and do what they were told. Brian had bought and nicked some very fast cars, including Mitsubishi Imprezas and Lancers which could stick to the road while taking speeds sometimes past 200kph. He literally knew every road back to Mitchelstown Cottage, every turn and every hill. Our displays for the Bradleys were totally choreographed. We'd see the brothers as we were racing along, mostly with the cops on our tail and they had taken to waving at us. Brian was thrilled. One night he told me to pull in and he started talking to Fatpuss. The next thing I knew he was sitting in the back of the car. "Who's the young fella? Is he your young lad?" he asked. Brian told him that I was The Lips and Fatpuss nodded his huge head. "Heard you've been doin' a few bits and you've a shed? Am I hearing right? The Boss said he'd meet you, said he might be up for doing a bit of business." Without even turning to look at him I knew that Brian was absolutely chuffed.

Apart from his armed robbery business, Marlo Hyland was far and above the undisputed crime boss over Finglas. In the absence of anyone more powerful, he had also secured the vast territory of Ballymun. While the Bradleys were his front men, he was the real top dog and my God did he know it. Legend had it that Hyland had taken out his own boss, Peter Psycho Judge, in a cool, calculated hit outside the Royal Oak Pub in Finglas in 1996, in order to take his throne. Judge had been nicknamed Psycho after he buried a man alive one night in a field because he was jealous of his good looks; he was seen as totally untouchable before Marlo plugged him. Marlo was a Finglas lad himself but had been involved in serious crime for years– probably since before I was born. They said he turned bad when his sister Julia was raped and murdered years before by her husband Michael Brady. When Brady got out of prison Marlo had tracked him down and assassinated him as payback. I actually remembered the story myself because I'd seen a graphic picture of Brady, shot in the head and slumped over the steering wheel of his car, on the front page of a newspaper. I remember being in a shop and women with prams talking about how the city had "gone to hell." The murder had sort of become Marlo's calling card and I would have ever expected to meet with the legendary gangster in my lifetime. But like many of the bizarre and dangerous roads I had been down since I first met Brian, an audience with the Godfather seemed like just another day's work.

Thankfully Brian had pumped me full of cocaine that morning and warned me not to speak unless I was spoken too. In hindsight I'm not really sure why he brought me at all, although I suspect I was there as some sort of fashion accessory. Many of the gangsters that inhabited the underworld had young boys with them although I don't believe they were all doing to them what Brian was doing to me. When Marlo turned his gaze to me and asked who I was and if I could be trusted, I at least knew to leave the talking to Brian. "This is The Lips. He's not my son but he is like my son." I shifted from foot to foot and glanced up at the boss. Marlo looked me up and down again. I couldn't help but notice his eyes. They were just like a shark's and they darted all over the room taking in everything. They were big but expressionless and they were everywhere. You could see he was thinking all the time. "So this is the young fella I've heard about. Can we trust him?" Marlo said. The room was very tense and Brian almost babbled as he assured him I was totally trustworthy and would do anything I was told. "I can trust The Lips with my life. I can absolutely assure you of that," he said.

There was another long silence before Marlo spoke again. I had taken one line too many of cocaine and feeling my jaw crunching, I concentrated on trying to stop it. Although the millennium was approaching, when I would turn 15, I still hadn't managed to grow very much so I must have looked like a child amongst them. Wayne was outside the pub keeping watch but Fatpuss had sat himself beside Marlo and was examining me with the same surgical precision of his boss. In the corner a shifty-looking character who had been introduced to us as Chicore was smoking and I could see he was grinning and enjoying the show.

"Chicore," Marlo called. "Get us drinks and whatever The Lips is having." I said I'd have a coke but had barely got the words out of my mouth when Marlo slammed his fist down on the table, and staring at me, said to Chicore, "He'll have a pint of Bulmers. We don't talk business with young fellas." Marlo kept staring at me with his cold dead blue eyes. "Put your fingers on the side of the table young fella." You could hear a pin drop in the room. I looked at Brian but he nodded for me to do it. I laid my hands flat along the table and felt the sticky remains of the pints from the night before under my sweating palms. Then I hung my fingers over the side of the table. I've no doubt that without the other coke surging through my veins I might have blinked or even creased my face as I waited for the big fists to come down on my hands; but with it, I had the courage to hold his stare. There was complete silence that seemed to go on forever until eventually Marlo threw back his head, opened his arms and said, "C'mere and give me a hug. You're a good young fella all right.'

CHAPTER 6

Brian and I dropped onto the stools in front of us and he slapped me across the back as the drinks arrived. "These drinks are on Paul Williams,' Marlo announced and everyone cracked up laughing, none more so than Brian, who held his ribs as he rolled around on the bar stool. Brian and I had been reading about the court case in which Marlo successfully sued the country's top crime correspondent Paul Williams. Williams, who worked for the *Sunday World* newspaper, akin to *Hello* magazine for the Irish criminal fraternity, had accused Marlo of being a drug dealer, which of course he was, but because Marlo had never been convicted, the newspaper was forced to pay him compensation. Marlo had put it around Finglas and Ballymun that the 100k had come directly from Williams' own pocket and that he was going to enjoy every penny of it.

Although we were now at least sitting down and my hands were firmly wrapped around a pint of cider rather than swinging over the side of the table, my nerves certainly weren't settled, and by the look of Brian I could see that his weren't either. Despite the fact that he was trying to look calm and sound cool, he was sweating buckets beside me and his leg was doing 90 on the floor. Before we had left the house Brian had confessed to me that he was worried. "What if he doesn't want to do business, The Lips? What if that is just made up? What if he wants to talk to me about selling smack on his patch without his permission, huh? Did you think of that? I bet you fuckin' didn't. But I have, I've thought about it. What if he's pissed that I was buying off Hinchon and not him. Did tha' even cross your mind ye thick fuck?" His voice become an accusatory shout by the end of it. I knew he didn't really want an answer, and all the way over to Finglas he had repeated his concerns. Now, as we were about to get down to business, I knew he wasn't feeling confident at all.

"So Brian, I hear ye have been doing a few jobs and that ye aren't half bad. I hear ye have a shed which I may be interested in using if we do some business." Beside me I could feel the tension drain from Brian. "I've a few jobs on meself at the moment and I'm looking for a premises." Marlo was an absolute master and I wondered whether anyone in the world had ever said no to him before and if so, which intensive care unit they had ended up in. Brian explained to Marlo the size and scale of the shed, what it could handle, how easily it could be accessed and finally, how well hidden it was from the road or from any other access point. "Sounds like you have yerself a partner," Marlo said, nodding to Fatpuss to shake hands with his new wingman.

There was more talk about fund-splitting and percentages and when everyone seemed satisfied, Marlo threw a couple of bags of coke onto the table and cut it into lines for everyone. The pints flowed and the atmosphere started to relax a bit. I didn't dislike Marlo despite his reputation but I was definitely afraid of him. He was sharp and he was quite funny but most

CHAPTER 6

of all he had this presence where you just knew he was the Boss. The talk eventually came around to Brian and his smack conviction, but instead of griping at him, Marlo was sympathetic and told him he would give him a good price in the future when he was ready to get back on the horse. "Best game in town my friend. You come to me when the heat is died down. I'll get you the best smack in Dublin at the best price."

Chicore stayed in the shadows and looked like he was brooding over something. The more cocaine he took, the more tense he appeared to get and it was pretty hard to miss that he had taken a total dislike to Brian. As the afternoon wore on and business turned to pleasure, he made a few remarks about Brian being a smack dealer and how he didn't like his company. I had to stifle a laugh that he was taking umbrage with Brian while at the same time working for the biggest smack dealer in Ireland. But the coke was making him very jumpy and he began staring at Brian and going on about "heroin scumbags" and how much he hated them. "Shut the fuck up, Chicore. Change the fuckin' record will ye," Fatpuss told him a few times, but it didn't seem to make much of a difference. Eventually Marlo gave Fatpuss a nod and he stood up and lifted Chicore up and onto his feet in one quick move. It was an elegant removal and Chicore was out the door before anyone had a chance to notice what was happening. A short while later everything wrapped up as quickly as it began. Marlo stood up, clapped his hands together and then extended a shake to Brian. "Nice doing business with you my friend," he said. "Fatpuss will be in touch."

On the way back to Mitchelstown Cottage Brian was talking 100 miles an hour. "Anything we want, The Lips. Did ye hear him? Anything. Guns, cars, men. Did ye hear him? Marlo fuckin' Hyland, can ye believe it. Marlo Hyland tellin' us 'anything yiz want'. We're gonna be busy The Lips. Bada bing. Bada boom."

I couldn't help but feel the excitement too. The mix of the coke and cider along with the thrill of being in the company of the Godfather of crime had made me feel like a real player. But the feeling of elation didn't last long. On the backroads at Kilshane Cross, Brian suddenly pulled the car over and the familiar sound of his zip made my heart sink. "C'mon. We haven't all day, The Lips. Get it done."

Back at Mitchelstown Cottage Brian was like a Duracell Bunny and made me go out and clean the shed so it would be ready for our new business partners. He paced the floors talking to himself while sniffing line after line of cocaine. A few hours later a car came up the drive and we looked out to see one of the blue Insignias outside the house. It was Fatpuss to tell us that Marlo wanted to apologise to Brian for the way his friend Chicore had treated him and that it wouldn't happen again. Brian looked as if he was about to explode with happiness. He went on and on and on about the meeting with Marlo and told me about it as if I hadn't been there at all.

"And then he shook my hand and he looked into me eye and he said, 'I look forward to doin' business with ye Brian'." I pretended to be impressed by the revelations. "The Lips, do ye know what this means. Do you know what it means? I'll have enough money soon and I can move to the country and to give it all up. Myself and Rita and Robyn and Conor, we'll be off to live in the country and you can have this, all this." Myself and Rita stole a glance at one another and at the same time we threw our eyes up to heaven. While I wasn't growing physically, I had certainly learned to be more cynical.

Days after the meeting with Marlo, Fatpuss was back at Mitchelstown Cottage, this time hammering out plans for a robbery on pub in north Dublin. Marlo had received a tip that the pub takings were pretty healthy on a particular night and that the manager would leave with them under his arm not long after the last customers had left. Fatpuss arrived in a Mitsubishi Gallant which he had stolen in the inner city somewhere. It was the car they were to use for the job and it was left in the shed in the meantime. I knew I'd be the one sent to burn it out afterwards and it seemed such a waste. It was a beautiful car. Fatpuss said that Wayne had been sent to watch the pub for a few weeks to confirmed how the manager left and which direction he went once he locked up. From the sofa I watched the television and pretended I wasn't listening but I could hear them making their plans at the kitchen table. "So we park around the corner and we are in the back with the guns, yeah?" I didn't want to turn around in case they realised I was eavesdropping but the voice was unmistakably Fatpuss's. "When we get the call from Wayne, who will be parked up across the road watching the door, we speed around the corner and surprise him. That way he'll drop the fuckin' bag in fright and won't put up any resistance. Has everyone got it? It's simple really." They went over it again and again. "We need to drive at him as fast as we can. Don't stop until the bumper is touching his shins. That way he'll get a fright and drop it. Got it? Have we got it?"

For the next few days Brian drove to and from to the pub practising the getaway route. From Glasnevin he sped out around the back of the Sunnybank Hotel into Ballymun, onto the M50 and around the back of Kilshane Cross back to Mitchelstown Cottage. Brian timed himself day and night until he was totally acquainted with the route and had it down to a cool 10 minutes. "I have to get this right or there won't be another time," he said. Back at the yard he'd pace up and down repeating the plan over and over in his head, checking and rechecking the car. He had a type of wood burner at the back where clothes or other evidence would be burned and he walked me up and down to it over and over again, showing me how best to torch gloves, balaclavas and bags. He checked there was enough petrol and bleach in the garage so they could wash themselves afterwards and destroy any forensic evidence should they be caught. High on stress, adrenaline and coke, he was like a powder keg, eventually working himself up into such a frenzy that he'd beat me. "You will get me caught you fuckin' fool. Do ye know what to do? How many times do I have to tell ye?" In a way I was so used to it at that stage that mostly I used to just try to cover my head and wait for it to end.

On the night of the job they met in the shed. They each had a balaclava and some gloves. Brian kept his rolled into a little skull cap until such time as he needed to pull it down over his face. I'd seen him do that before. There was a strange atmosphere, a mixture of excitement and anticipation. Brian was coked up and chewing his gums like crazy. After getting a phone call from Wayne to say he was in place, they left at 2am . I waited. My job was to make sure the shed doors were open for them when they came back and to burn the clothes. Within about 30 minutes they were back, high on success and full of praise for one another. "That was so fuckin' easy," Brian told me later. "So easy. Wayne rings us and tells us he was out and walking down the road. We ploughed the car at him and between the glare of the lights and the noise of the brakes he nearly shit himself. We jumped out with the pieces but he just handed us the bag and that was it. I put me foot to the floor along the exact route we practised." Brian was delighted with himself but I don't think he got much money. There seemed to be quite a few in for a cut of it and of course Marlo was getting the lion's share.

Brian hung onto the car for three days. I went out to the shed a few times when nobody was looking and admired it until Brian told me to burn it out at the lanes by Dolly Heffernan's pub. The Mitsubishi was beautiful and felt so good to drive even though I needed to sit on two of the cushions from the couch in the living room because the wheel was so high up. I poured petrol around the inside of the car and then lit a sock and threw it in. Then I ran like hell because cars explode really quickly.

The next job I can remember them doing was a bookies which they hit during the day. I was at home full of coke waiting for them to come back in a stolen Pajero. I was standing in the yard when I heard it flying up the road. When they arrived they were very excited. They said the woman behind the counter decided to be brave and didn't want to give them the money, but Fatpuss had grabbed her and she'd changed her mind. They always rested for a couple of weeks between jobs while things settled down. But it wasn't long before they were on another big one, a cash-in-transit robbery of a bank in Finglas. It was again Wayne's job to scope the place out and find out which times the van would arrive with the cash in a big sealed box. While they tried all sorts of things, like unbreakable locks on the boxes, and dye to destroy the notes if they were smashed open, Fatpuss had mastered ways of getting around the security systems and was an expert at opening up the sealed containers. "Just leave it to me," he would say sagely whenever anyone started stressing about it.

CHAPTER 6

Brian and Fatpuss tried to teach me as they went along. "Ye have to drive at people like you're going to knock them down, kiddo. Security workers carrying cash for a living won't be as shocked as ordinary businesspeople. They are on higher alert, do ye get me? So ye really need to drive fast. But we don't want to kill them so you have to get the knack of it. Drive hard enough to get them to drop the box. But not hard enough to kill dem." It felt like we were in a classroom.

The car was in the shed with the plates changed and I watched them as they all got rigged out in their balaclavas and gloves. The stove I used to destroy evidence was a free standing, pot-bellied one, like you'd see in a pub. After the bank job in Finglas, I watched them separating the money from the car and the guns. Fatpuss washed in petrol and then took off in his truck towards Drogheda with the box of cash. I think they made around 35k from that one. Later that day Brian got a phone call from Marlo to congratulate us on a job well done. "Tell The Lips he's comin' along good," he said.

The jobs became fast and frequent: the Bank of Ireland in Finglas, the Bookies and the Shanty Pub in Blanchardstown village, Myos in Castleknock. They were running a 100% success rate which pleased Marlo no end. In his spare time Brian was out with me on the road running a "legitimate" pallet collection service in the Dyna van; really just a cover to of scope for opportunities. He always had to make sure he kept Marlo in the loop. I remember one night he robbed a factory and stole a load of leather furniture. The following morning Brian rang Marlo and we dropped a large chocolate brown sofa up to his house. It was as busy as ever and I had little or no time for anything else in my life.

I saw Ma less and less. My older brother and my sisters knew a bit of what was going on with Brian; they certainly knew his reputation. Louise and Niamh were constantly trying to take me aside, warning me to stay away from him telling me to come home, but I knew myself I was a lost cause. Ma just seemed to hope for the best. When a small article had appeared in one of the papers about Brian receiving his suspended sentence for the heroin, Ma had come up to the cottage to demand I went home with her. But Brian spun her a yarn that he had been tricked and that he had been stupid. He told her that there was no way he had willingly got his own Da involved in anything to do with smack and blamed the other two Peters for dragging him into their mess. "Mrs O'Callaghan, I cannot explain to ye how much I fuckin' hate drugs. Excuse my language. It's just tha' it makes me so angry to think I was dragged into tha'. I really hate drugs. I wouldn't have dem near me or near him." He looked at me, but once Ma took her gaze off him he sneaked me a wink. "I'm so embarrassed about it all Mrs O'Callaghan. My own Da and Ma have been forced to sell up their house and move because they are so ashamed. I would never have done this to them. I promise you. It was the other two. They were doing it and they landed me in it too." It really was an Oscar-winning performance. I think Ma ended up almost feeling sorry for Brian. He was like that. He was very persuasive with people.

When I did get to see her, Ma would give me money for my keep. I didn't realise that Brian had been getting at her about the cost of me living at the house and he told her he'd been picking up all my bills for clothes and food and everything else on top of my wages. I was shocked when I found out much later that he had asked her to sign over guardianship to him so he could claim my child's allowance. After visiting her Brian would ask me for whatever money Ma had given me, and I would hand it over. I don't think I actually ever earned any more from the illegal stuff with Brian than I did from the milk rounds but having me with him all the time meant he could control everything about me. He would take me out to buy me clothes. He hated me wearing tracksuits and hoodies. He'd make me buy trousers and shirts and stuff. I'd often be sitting there in the cottage dressed like I was off to Hogwart's and he'd be cutting up lines of coke for me. It was all so fucked up. He'd be telling me I was his son one minute then beating me and forcing me the next. I took some terrible beatings and assaults in that shed. That was the worst of all. I would dread the moments when his face would change and he'd tell me to pull up the shutter.

Me Da died in the summer of 2000. His health had been deteriorating for a long time from the constant drinking. I'd only really seen him a few times a year since I had started working for Brian. I visited him once or twice when I was in Ballymun but he didn't like Brian at all. I'd given him some money but the bond we had when I was a child had gone. As I got older I could see what a chronic alcoholic he was and it was very hard to see the way he was living . I had been on a rare visit at Ma's the night Da took bad. I'd gone out to meet a few of my friends and was walking back to the house when I saw Ma and Niall coming down the driveway. They told me they were going to the hospital and that Da was sick. I went inside to bed but when Ma woke me the next morning she told me that Da had died and that Brian was downstairs. "He's going to take you off to get you ready, Joseph," she said. "You go now and get yourself kitted out. We will have to look nice for your Da."

Brian took me off then to buy me a suit and dropped me at the Church in Ballymun on the morning of the funeral. I was drowsy and out of it because he had pumped me full of Valium, but I do remember all these men dressed in all these colours coming in to do salutes over the coffin. My sister Louise, who was dressed in her army uniform, stayed outside the church and wouldn't come in until the men had gone. After he was buried, Brian arrived to collect me and took me back to Mitchelstown Cottage where I just sat in front of the television feeling completely numb. That evening there was a knock on the door and Brian told me that I had visitors. It was Marlo Hyland and the Bradley brothers who had come to pay their respects. They all walked in looking very sombre and gave me

CHAPTER 6

a big hug and told me they were sorry to hear about me Da. Later after I went to bed, Brian came into my room and ruffled my covers as if he was trying to tuck me into bed. "We're your family now The Lips. Me and the lads. We are the ones here for ye. Ye don't need anyone else. Just us." He turned at the door and in the darkness I heard him whisper, "Family."

CHAPTER 7

"When you don't get betrayed… with that old Judas kiss… Oh my mama told me… there'd be days like this…"

Marlo Hyland swayed from side to side as he led the room in singing and drowned out Van Morrison for the umpteenth time. Stubbing out his cigarette in an ashtray, he bent down to the table in front of him with a rolled-up 50 euro note and hoovered up a massive line of coke. When he lifted his head he looked over toward me and roared over the music, "C'mon The Lips, get it into ye." *"There'll be days like this,"* the throng chanted and clapped their hands above their heads.

The thing with coke is it makes your nose run like hell and has you so hyper that even if you do stop talking for a minute, your jaw keeps going, grinding your teeth like a Magimix. Mine were beginning to feel sore. I'd probably been on the sniff for 24 hours but I didn't care; the atmosphere was electric and although we were in a shed at the back of the Bradleys' house, I felt like a Vegas high-roller. *"Days like this…"* The music was like our anthem, the same song that Fatpuss and Brian used to always play at full volume after speeding across the backroads of Dublin to Mitchelstown Cottage, following a successful ram raid or a cash-in-transit robbery.

I took a huge gulp from my can of cider and ran my sleeve across my face, wiping my nose as I did. By the time I had taken two steps to the table, where a perfect line of white powder was waiting for me, I was running like a tap again. Marlo threw his head back and laughed out loud. "*Days like this…*" he roared into my face as I lowered my head to the table and sucked in every grain of powder. I came back up for air to a huge cheer. "Go wan The Lips." I knew most of the faces: there was Brian's pal Peter Joyce, the milkman who'd been done with him for the smack, Eamon Dunne, one of Marlo's dealers who'd brought most of the coke, and some of the lads from the Filthy Fifty, who were slugging back beer and groping girls in mini-skirts and high-heeled boots.

I saw Wayne talking in a corner with John Daly and Deccie Curran. He was going in and out of the shed and through the house to the front to keep an eye on the unmarked patrol car sitting outside on Cappagh Road. "Tango One in place," he'd announce each time he came back, sending Marlo into heaps of laughter. Fatpuss was on the decks playing requests that varied from The Prodigy to Flashdance. I couldn't see Brian but as I scanned the crowd for him, I saw a sweaty-looking Sticky Vicky making her way in from the garden. She walked back over to her boyfriend, who we had nicknamed The Muppet and put her arm around him, just as Brian came in the same door after her. Brian looked over at me, ran his tongue across his lips and winked towards Sticky Vicky.

It was a big night but nothing special. They regularly held impromptu raves like this either at the Bradleys or in the shed at Mitchelstown Cottage where there was a snooker table and a dart board. Some of the guys Marlo supplied from Blanchardstown arrived and a crew from the north inner city along with a load of girls they knew, some of whom they had picked up on the way. There was champagne, vodka, beer and mountains of white. Every so often Fatpuss would put a song on the decks and everyone would put their arms around one another and sway from side to side as they sang along. Outside on the street the undercover Garda car sat watching the house all night, but nobody gave a fuck – not until the paranoia kicked in, that was.

Marlo was the first to start. "Hey Brian, is that your mate Strats out there? He really has one fuckin' hard-on for me and the lads. Hope yer not singing." Brian laughed and told Fatpuss to turn the music up, but he wasn't paying any attention. "Ye think it's fuckin' funny do ye?" Marlo was turning nasty although you never knew if he was joking or serious. Brian hated that he was still an outsider when it came to Marlo's crew. Like some of the lads in the Filthy Fifty, he was really only hired help, but liked to think of himself as being part of the inner circle. I knew at moments like this when Marlo showed that blood is thicker than water that Brian would be raging at being ridiculed so publicly, even through the haze of coke and beer and whiskey . "Course I don't. He's only a cunt," said Brian, his face turning purple. The music seemed to lower and the shed went quiet while Marlo held Brian's stare. Without turning his eyes he pointed over towards me. "Ye better make sure The Lips knows what to do if he's lifted. Ye hear me?" My nose felt hot and wet. "He knows," Brian said almost meekly, looking nothing like the monster who pummelled his fists and feet into me at will. "The Lips knows." With that, Marlo smiled, punched him in the left shoulder and spun around towards Fatpuss, ordering him to play another round of Van Morrison.

Brian let the party rev up again and then nodded over at me. I knew it was time to go. I knocked back my drink and we slipped out the shed door and round the side of the house to the front garden, where we put up our hoods as we headed for the car. "I'm drivin'," Brian said and I threw him the keys. All the way home to Mitchelstown Cottage he ranted and raved to me never to let him down and if that cop Strats ever lifted me, I was to say nothing, touch nothing and do nothing. My jaw was aching so I opened and closed my mouth and rubbed the sides of my face as we drove at speed through Finglas and out towards Kilshane Cross. The next thing I remember was the back of his fist coming at me full force and the warm sensation as blood poured down my nose onto my lap. "Are ye fuckin' listenin' to me?" I nodded, trying to catch the blood in my T-shirt before it stained the car seat. The fist came down again and again and again as that all-too-familiar demon engulfed Brian.

When he got back to Mitchelstown Cottage he was shaking and foaming at the mouth. He barely took the time to stop the engine before dragging me out of the car across the driver's seat and onto the concrete yard. He tried to stamp on my head and I rolled around in the darkness trying to protect myself. "Get in to the shed," he hissed, grabbing me by my hair, my ear and my neck and finally almost pulling my arm out of its socket. The shed's metal door slammed shut and he grabbed me around the throat, his eyes only inches from mine and red with rage. "I'll fuckin' show ye to yawn when I'm talkin' to ye."

The first time he brought the crowbar down it was inches from my left ear. The metal rang like a church bell as it hit concrete. The next time it came full force at my shoulder and as I turned in pain it connected with my side, my back, my legs, my butt. Each blow harder than the last. My insides screamed in pain and I wondered again if I would die that night on the cold concrete floor. I closed my eyes and tried to block out what was happening but the coke was racing through my veins. "Do ye want me? Do ye want this? I'd only be breakin' ye in, ye fuckin' faggot," he roared, grabbing his crotch and pushing himself against me. I hated when Brian started that. I'd take a beating any day. When he was finished he was exhausted. He dropped the crowbar and pulled open the door of the shed. Morning had broken and sunlight flooded in. "I'm makin' breakfast," he said. "Do ye want a cup of tea?"

Despite the turmoil and the chaos of my existence, life just seemed to limp on at Mitchelstown Cottage. Over the years I have learned that one man's normality is another's insanity and it really takes a lot to break the human spirit. Rita and Brian fought constantly and even when he wasn't beating her they would be bickering all the time. I felt sorry for her and the kids. She just didn't have a strong enough personality to deal with him and he bullied her constantly. I stepped in as often as I could. I took beating after beating for her so she could usher Robyn and Conor away from the violence. She spent a lot of time at her mother's house or with friends and would often go into town in the morning and come back laden with stuff for the house. She called it retail therapy. Brian had been so tight-fisted with his money when I first met her and he even made her account for buying a packet of cigarettes. He had become more generous in his desire to fit in, however. Marlo and his crew lavished money on their women and he wanted to do the same. It was nothing to the lads to hand out 5,000 euro or to go on a shopping spree at Brown Thomas. They all loved the Louis Vuitton bags and the Jo Malone candles and the really expensive makeup they sell at the counters there. I remember Rita liked Alexander McQueen. She always dressed very well and liked to wear jewellery and drive a nice car but I remember thinking none of those things were worth the awful life she had with Brian.

And she didn't know the half of it. While she was painfully aware of the violence, I think she at least thought he was faithful to her. But in truth, Brian was playing the field and had been since I had first met him. Even when Rita had been pregnant he'd been seeing a few other women. Sometimes he'd leave me in the car and go into a house for an hour and come back out full of crude remarks about what had been done to him inside. There was another house we regularly went to for parties with Marlo and the crew which was fitted out with a waterbed shaped like a love heart. It was like something off *Love Island* but there was nothing romantic about it. The lads would order in a load of brassers for the night and they'd sniff coke and pass the women around. They'd throw wads of notes around the place so they'd feel like real gangsters. A lot of the girls injected the coke which would be left out everywhere you looked and drink and shag all night long.

At one point Brian was having sex with two sisters and he'd laugh and say he was as good as The General, another one of his heroes in life. The General — aka Martin Cahill — was a legendary Irish criminal who'd been shot dead in 1994 after a long career giving two fingers to the authorities. He was a famous robber and had staged some huge art heists in his time, including the theft of a Rubens and other priceless works from

CHAPTER 7

Russborough House in Wicklow. Amongst other things, he was notorious for living with two sisters, who were happy to share him. I don't think either of the sisters who were sleeping with Brian were aware that he was with the other. I believe that it was the allure of the drugs rather than his charm that had got him into their beds. Rita certainly didn't know that Brian was abusing me as regularly as clockwork at this point. He thought nothing of pulling in to the side of a quiet road and pushing my head down onto his lap. Even worse things had started happening in the shed. I was taking more and more coke and pills and drink to block it all out.

Brian was very into himself. He spent a lot of time perfecting the image he portrayed to the world, but like many things in Brian's world it was pretty odd. His uniform was a pair of corduroy trousers coupled with a crisp white shirt and a cardigan. Sometimes he wore Aran jumpers and he had a collection of shoes the likes of which I had never seen. Most of them were leather brogues with a high heel. From very early on he had also started to control what I wore and he began to dress me in identical clothes to him. If we were going out he'd make sure that I was wearing the exact same style as him so I looked like his little clone. I felt seriously uncomfortable in the gear, and because I was so small I looked like a real nerd. Most people thought I was his son and even those who knew I wasn't just accepted it. In the underworld of gangland crime, many criminals have younger sidekicks who accompany them everywhere and do as they are told. They see them as their little projects and no doubt many of them, like me, become immersed in this shady world before they even realise it. It was only when I was out dealing his drugs or scoping out places with him that I was allowed wear my own tracksuits and runners.

Looking back I would say that while Rita liked the material comforts she gained from her relationship with Brian, she was probably really struggling with the rest of it. When she went out she looked great but at home she often sat around in her nightdress smoking all day long. Rita loved having me around and she never wanted me to leave. "Ah Joey you don't want to go home do ye? This is yer home. Stay here with us, sit with me, we'll have a movie and popcorn tonight how is tha'," she'd often say if I suggested a visit to Ma's. The kids were pretty scared of Brian and they would always come looking for me if they sensed trouble. I was like a big brother to them which made me feel like I could never leave them. I used to make sure they were clean and tidy and fed because sometimes Rita didn't have it in her to get up and make dinner. I'd always make Robyn a little packed lunch for school and usually drop her there and collect her if I was around. Sometimes the kids reminded me of myself when I was younger and while I have so many regrets about my years with Brian, making an effort for these kids isn't one of them.

Brian had steered clear of dealing smack since his run-in with the law but his sense of community spirit stopped there.

CHAPTER 7

We were still selling coke to many of our old customers and a raft of new ones he had gathered. I was pretty much left in charge of that end of the business while he went out on the armed robberies. Despite being promised a good deal on Marlo's product, Brian had managed to source it more cheaply. To keep the Big Fella happy, he was buying one key off him and another six from one of his original suppliers in the south of the city. Brian always looked after the pennies as well as the pounds and told me to do the same even though neither found their way to me. I was doing most of the selling during the day. I laugh now when I hear these big reports talking about the "uberisation" of coke, as if it's a new thing that customers can call for it like a takeaway. Sure we were years ahead of our time delivering it right to people's work places. I'd spend my day driving between supermarkets and bookies' offices and then into town where I'd meet blokes in car parks. Some of them had big jobs and there was one guy who was actually a chief executive in a big company who would be looking for it every day. There were dockworkers, employees at Dublin airport, and even a copper that Brian knew who was buying it off him.

Coke had really, really exploded in Dublin at that stage. It was the beginning of the noughties and I suppose ordinary people were starting to make lots of money. Guys who were working in the construction industry like brick layers and plasterers were all going mad for the sniff and I could literally have been out 24/7 selling it. We were still using the pallet collection business as our cover and even the guys in the pallet yards were queuing up to buy it off us. I would say we were clearing about five grand a day with the coke and more at the weekend. The place had literally gone stone-mad on white and there were lads killing one another all over the city for a slice of the action. It was like a gold-rush and everyone was trying to stake their territory. Added to the mix was the fact that everybody who was selling it was also taking it themselves; this made for a very tense atmosphere.

There was definitely a new violence in the air that I don't think had been as prevalent before. My old neighbours from Blanchardstown were leading the charge . In the years since I had hung out with Adam Coates, his brother Shane and his pal Stephen Sugg – the Westies – had gained a notorious reputation. The newspaper was crammed full of gangster stories every week and Brian always made sure to buy it to read up on what was happening. We could usually work out who the characters were even when no names were mentioned; one of the headlines screamed: "The new Psycho." This was a reference to Shane, who had given me my first taste of hand-break turns when he'd taken me and Adam for a spin. The nickname had come from Marlo's old boss, Peter Judge.

I had only seen Coates a few times since I had started working with Brian. We'd nod to one another but I gave him a wide berth otherwise. Around the time I was starting work with Brian on the milk float, he and his pal Stephen Sugg had been released from prison for a second time and had quickly assembled a large gang of criminals and addicts to bag and sell their gear. I had heard all the stories and Brian had talked about them incessantly. "But what was he really like," he'd ask me as we made our way around the housing estates. "What did he want ye to call him?" I always found the questions odd but looking back I can see that he was a bit in awe of them, particularly because of their fearsome reputation and the way they taxed others who worked on their patches. They had shot dead a drug dealer called Pascal Boland when he tried to trade on their patch, tortured a young fella who went out with one of their sisters and beaten a drug addict to a pulp. And these were just some of the things going around about them. Some of the stories were so gory it was hard to believe they were true. They were known to knife addicts who owed them as little as fifty quid, often leaving them mutilated. They regularly attacked the homes of junkies' family members and intimidated anyone who tried to go to the police. They were so notorious that public meetings were held about them and every few days there were stories about them in the papers. My Ma was terrified of them and her and Niall actually sold up in Blanchardstown partly because of them and moved back to Ballymun shortly after my Da died. I don't think they were alone.

Closer to home, Marlo Hyland and some of his crew had similarly terrifying reputations and I was always worried that

Brian would piss him off. While the lads all seemed to like me they didn't really warm to Brian and I could tell that him and Wayne Bradley in particular had a bit of a personality clash. Sometimes Brian thought he was too clever and things like undercutting Marlo by buying gear off someone else didn't seem the best idea to me. "Would ye not be better to just get the whole lot off him?" I'd suggest, but any questioning of Brian's authority was likely to send him into a black rage so I avoided the topic most of the time. Brian and I were different. I didn't have that same love affair with money that he had, and still worked for little more than my bed and board. I did think that it was short sighted to piss off the Big Fella for the sake of a few quid.

Things had really come full circle since I'd been with Brian. The slowdown after his arrest for smack-dealing was just a brief respite and we were back on a mad treadmill of work, work, work. The only difference this time was that cocaine was the drug.

Brian's other great obsession was a criminal known as John Gilligan who was always in the news around then. He was very famous in Ireland because his gang had been responsible for the murder of the journalist Veronica Guerin, who had been writing about him. Gilligan had been a cannabis dealer but had hit the big time very rapidly in the mid-1990s. He was everything Brian wanted to be. The fact that he and his crew had been all rounded up after the Guerin killing didn't seem to bother him. Instead he went on and on about how Gilligan had provided the blueprint to how to get things done. "Gilligan kept buying more and selling more. That's the secret to it. And look at how he got his place in the country. That's the way to do it, The Lips."

Gilligan had famously bought and developed an equestrian centre in County Kildare where he and his wife Geraldine had planned to host big events and mix with the horsey set. But that all had come a cropper after Guerin was shot dead by a gunman on the Naas Road and the whole country found out who Gilligan was. He was followed to the UK and extradited back to Ireland where he was acquitted of the murder in the Special Criminal Court but sentenced to 28 years for importing drugs, the longest jail term every handed down for drug offences. Members of his gang had turned supergrass and others had also been convicted. But for Brian it was all about the big house and the holidays to Sandy Lane in Barbados and the flash cars. He wanted all that and he was determined to follow in John Gilligan's footsteps to unimaginable wealth.

To build his drug business he stole everything he could from factories in the industrial estates around Blanchardstown and the airport, north into County Meath and west to County Kildare. One night he even broke into Fort Lucan, the kids outdoor adventure playground, and stole nearly €15k from the tills and the safe. He was so confident that he told me he hung around and played on some of the rides before making his getaway. "We need to buy more and sell more, The Lips," he'd say when he came home with his loot. "I'm just investing in all our futures." The shed could be full of anything from Christmas trees to crateloads of nappies, it didn't really matter to Brian once he was earning. He sold a lot of the grocery stuff to Paddy Harte in Finglas who sold knock-off stuff to women living off the social welfare from a van beside his house . Working class areas like that had their own black economy. Sometimes you would see an entire neighbourhood going around in designer tracksuits or fake Burberry scarves or whatever had recently been nicked. Smuggled cigarettes were sold under the counters and booze at Christmas time. All the robbers knew Paddy and he'd drive a hard bargain for anything with a short shelf-life, like meat or other food items. As well as robbery, Brian was also making a good wedge on "ringer cars", when he'd buy an engine and then rob a car to match. Depending on the model he could pull 10,000 euro from one of those.

While the honeymoon period was over with Marlo, we were still partying hard with his gang and Brian was doing big jobs with Fatpuss and Wayne whenever he was asked. The jobs for Marlo were still very important, but Brian wasn't too happy sharing the spoils with an executive director of operations who never got his hands dirty. He had started giving out about him. "That stupid prick does nothin' but sit on his arse and I hand him over my hard-earned money. Fuck tha'. Who does he think he is?"

CHAPTER 7

Of course it was very clear who Marlo was but Brian seemed to be losing sight of that and that was beginning to worry me. I'd try to jolly him along. "Yeah but nobody will touch ye because you are seen as one of Marlo's crew," I'd say, but there was no talking to him. Together they must have hit the cash-in-transit van at Finglas village three times in a row in exactly the same way. It was like Ground Hog Day. While Brian got on okay with Fatpuss, he didn't like Wayne. And Wayne didn't like him. I think they were probably quite alike and Brian was convinced he was touting to the cops. He had, of course, continued to do this himself even after he got his suspended sentence.

One day Wayne rang to tell Brian that he was wanted on a job involving the armed robbery of two garages. He had an insider, a woman who knew the lay of the land, so he needed to meet to work out arrangements. He rang again the next morning to say the meet was on at a fast foot outlet in a north-side shopping centre later that day. "Get yer jacket The Lips. You are comin' with me. This is how it's done." We travelled in convoy, myself and Brian in the first car and the Bradleys following behind. Just as we pulled into the car park there was a screech of tyres and two cars blocked us in. I thought at first we were going to get shot, but realised instead they were unmarked cop cars. We couldn't move and were ordered out of the car and down onto the ground. At least eight armed coppers surrounded us and kept their guns trained on us while afternoon shoppers looked on in shock. I hoped against hope that nobody who knew Ma was watching.

In the ensuing drama the Bradleys got away, but the cops separated myself and Brian and took us to different stations. I was thrown into a cell and left to consider my situation. Then the door opened and in walked the cop they called Strats, the one who seemed to have made it his mission to nab Marlo and the Bradleys. He was huge, standing well over 6 foot 3 and he leaned into my face. "So you're the young fella everyone is talking about," he said, grinning but not smiling. "Why don't you fuck off?" I roared, spitting in his face. His name was Detective Sergeant Kevin Stratford and he was feared and revered in equal measures. "Oh I don't think so, little boy," another officer said, walloping me across the face with a hand like a shovel. "I'm tellin' you fuckin' nothing" I said. "I'm underage. I want to go home." Strats stormed out of the cell and minutes later two uniformed coppers came in to take me to an interview room where he was waiting for me. I stood my ground refusing to go and when they tried to drag me I kicked and punched and wriggled and roared like they were giving me a hiding. I'm sure my protests could be heard all over the station.

By the time they plonked me into the plastic chair in front of Strats in the small interview room, I was practically hoarse from roaring at them. The big detective leaned over the desk. "What age are you now? 16? What are you doin' with this lot Joey?" I didn't reply. "You know Marlo Hyland? Fatpuss

Bradley? Wayne Bradley?" he asked me, pausing after each name for effect. "Never heard of 'em," I told him. "Are you sure? You want to think about that?" he said, repeating each name even slower this time. "I'm 100% sure mister, never heard of any of dem in me life." With that he stood up and took a handful of pictures out of a drawer and started to pin them to a white board on the wall. He moved at a snail's pace, pulling them out one after another like a poker player revealing his hand. I nearly fainted but tried not to show my shock. There was me and Marlo Hyland, me and Fatpuss Bradley, me and Anto Spratt, me talking to John Daly, me in the garden of the Bradley house leaning over the wall with Wayne. The cops had obviously been watching us for months.

"I've been watching you... The Lips... You think you're a big man in Ballymun, well you won't come down onto my patch and act like that," Strats said, emphasising that he knew my nickname. "But you and I can help each other out." I have to say I admired him and his courage. The lads were all afraid of him and they knew he was on their tail all the time. But I couldn't talk to him. Instead I chose a spot on the wall to stare at just as Brian had taught me, and started to shut out the voices in the room. For hours I said nothing, keeping my eyes fixed on the little crack where the pockmark of a nail was still visible. After a while they got fed up and they threw me back in the cell. I gave them Billy's number and he came and got me out. Just as I walked out of the station I heard a cheer erupt down the road and I saw the Bradleys and Brian driving towards me. "I told them ye wouldn't say anything, The Lips. Yer a good lad," Brian said, opening the back door and hugging me as I clambered in. Fatpuss turned from the front seat. "The Big Fella said to tell you he is proud of ye."

I wasn't sure exactly how the lads knew I had kept my mouth shut but I found out later that they knew someone in one of the adjoining cells who'd heard me giving Strats as good as I got. They drove me straight to the Castle Pub in Finglas that night where we played a scene straight out of *A Bronx Tale* to celebrate the fact that I hadn't been a rat. News travelled all over the pub and customers I didn't even know came over with glasses of vodka and pints of cider for me. All you had to do to be a hero was to say nothing. As the coke flowed and they toasted me again and again, I felt an enormous sense of belonging and sang my heart out with the rest. *"When it's not always raining...There'll be days like this."*

There is no doubt that Brian's violence was steadily increasing the more money he made, and he began to put us under more and more stress . By the end of 2001 he had become harder and harder to read. He was beating me and Rita more regularly and more severely. No matter how much money he was making it was never enough. He could have a brilliant day, pulling in thousands on the coke and topping that up with a good night's robbery, but he would still come home and kick me around the yard, or worse. He was constantly on the phone but he had become much more secretive in front of me. I wasn't stupid; I knew he was giving the cops info on the lads and playing his constant game of chess to keep just ahead of the law.

Brian was loyal to no one. He was like a crafty fox from a children's story who was always plotting and scheming and who just couldn't change his nature. I was at home one night with Rita and the kids and it was dark and lashing with rain outside. Brian was out. We were settling in to watch the telly when we heard his car on the pebbles outside before he burst through the back door looking deranged.

He started talking to himself and rooting through the drawers in the kitchen before eventually finding a couple of torches and handing one to me and one to Rita. He ordered us outside into the rain and marched us through the field to a ditch where he told us to find the gear. I knew we hadn't a hope of finding anything in the pitch dark and the rain but he was roaring and screaming at us to keep looking. I was dripping wet by the time he let me go back to the house. He was seething, but as we dried ourselves off I realised that he and Wayne had helped his milkman colleague Peter Joyce hide some cannabis he had bought. Joyce was supposed to be his friend but Brian walked all over him. Brian and Wayne had gone back, nicked the cannabis and buried it in our ditches. But when Brian had gone out to get it, it had disappeared. He was sure that Wayne was responsible as he was the only other person who knew its location.

He was absolutely furious and bent on revenge. "Keep looking. Keep fuckin' looking." Rita and I were drenched, miserable and scared by the time he eventually gave up. The following morning he was up early and pacing the floors trying to decide what to do. Joyce was out for his blood and he was out for Wayne's. Eventually he decided he would burn out both their cars and get them to blame each other while staying out of the loop. "Fuckin' gobshites the two of dem," he said. I wasn't so sure.

Joyce fell for it and Brian managed to convince him that the whole double-cross was the work of Wayne, but Wayne didn't buy the story that Joyce had torched his Nissan. The row rumbled on until eventually Marlo called a meeting and the two of them agreed to park their dispute for the sake of business. The hatchet was buried but neither Brian nor Wayne would ever trust one another again.

Christmas came and went. My presents and the kids' were left out together. I got a PlayStation and a wrestling game I was looking for. I got a few hours to play with it on the couch while Rita cooked the dinner but people want coke on Christmas Day too so most of my day was spent driving around the city with bags of white. Ma rang and she was really upset that I wasn't coming home. I told her that I was going up to see Brian's Ma in Drogheda but she cried and told me that she would always be there for me. Brian eventually took the phone from me, wished her a Happy Christmas and hung up.

CHAPTER 7

A few weeks later on the day of my 17th birthday, Brian was in party mood and decided we were taking the day off no matter what. He wanted to celebrate me "becoming a man". We dressed up in our matching gear and headed over to Inchicore to meet up with the guy who was undercutting Marlo with the coke.

He lived in a grim and dark flat in St Michael's Estate and when we got there two of his friends were already there drinking cans of beer and sniffing. They were two IRA lads who had known my Da. We got talking about the Concerned Parents and they told me a few funny stories about Da that I hadn't heard. I settled in for the party. We sniffed a bit of coke and threw back the cans and then we went over to the local pub for a few rounds of pool and darts.

We went back to the flat later and a few women showed up. Brian was out of it, telling me that he loved me and how proud he was of me. At one point he called everyone to order by clinking a fork on his pint glass and stood up to make a big long speech about me and how I had never let him down and how he could trust me with his life. "He's like me son. He is me son," he slurred. "He means the world to me. And I would give him the shirt off me back." Everyone was hugging me and Brian and the coke flowed.

At about three or four in the morning Brian had enough and we drove back to Mitchelstown Cottage. I was so grateful he hadn't stopped off in a layby on the way so he could force me to relieve him. But we had only just walked in the house when he turned on me in the sitting room. I had absolutely no idea what I was supposed to have done wrong but he was spitting in my face and telling me I'd never disrespect him again. He started punching and kicking me and wrestling me around the floor. I tried not to scream because I knew Rita and the kids were asleep and I really didn't want to frighten them. "Come on faggot," he sneered at me. "You want it, don't you?" Brian started tugging at his trousers and I tried to get to my feet and scramble away. He usually restricted these attacks to the shed so no one else could hear, but that night he did it right in the house while the kids slept. Anyone could have walked in at any time. He kept his hand clamped so tightly around my mouth that I could barely breathe let alone cry out.

When he was finished he lay down on the couch and told me to lie on the floor beside him. Then he slept. In the morning I was really upset, not only from the physical injuries. To me Brian had crossed a line in the sand. If he was willing to do that right under the noses of his family, then he was capable of doing anything.

I was also really upset that he had done it to me on my birthday – as if it was okay on any other day of the year. I reasoned I'd done nothing to deserve it, and I told him I was going home to my Ma. "And this time I'm not comin' back. Not ever," I told him. "You can go and fuck yourself now." He flipped again and this time went to the kitchen drawer and took out a knife. He pinned me to the sofa and held the knife to my throat. "You're not going anywhere, The Lips. Yer stayin' here with me. And with Rita." Just then Rita walked in and he loosened his grip on my neck. "The Lips doesn't want to babysit for us tonight, Rita love. I'm just tellin' him we want to go out." Rita looked shocked and said nothing but his strength had gone. I pushed him off while he was distracted. "I'm goin' and I'm not comin back," I said again. I could feel Rita's pleading eyes boring into me but I dropped my gaze to the floor and walked out.

I must have been a mess when I arrived at Ma's but she just prepared a bed for me and told me to go and lie down. Ma was back in me Da's old council house and although it had been done up, it was still familiar and comforting. Niall was gone. Their relationship hadn't survived their shattered dreams of Blanchardstown and the new life they had hoped for. There was no animosity, however, and he would remain close to all of us until the day he died.

Ma had remained the named tenant on me Da's house after she had essentially given it to him when she moved out and tried to make a go of things in the UK after their break up . When he died she had set about making it her family home again. The house was in an awful state and she had used the money from the sale in Blanchardstown to have it completely gutted and refurbished, fitting new windows and even re-plastering the walls which had punch holes in them. Even after all of that, and painting it from top to toe, she said she could still smell the smoke which she reckoned had seeped into the concrete. She had the house lovely. Niamh was still living at home and Natalie still had her lovely pleasant personality despite now being a teenager. Everyone was thrilled that they were back in Ballymun

Ma knew something had happened but she gave me loads of space as I settled back down into life away from Brian. I stayed in for a good few weeks, lolling around on the couch watching telly and doing nothing for the first time in years. My sleep pattern was all over the place so sometimes I'd be up all night and in bed all day, it just depended on how I was feeling. I switched off my mobile phone and then one day I went out and got a new one with a brand new number. I still had plenty of friends in Ballymun despite not living there in years. My childhood friends, my old pals from the Towers, heard I was back and they started calling to the door and we were soon hanging out. We had our girls that knocked around with us and while we would drink cans and listen to music, that was really the worst of what we got up to. Sometimes I'd see familiar faces from the days I was selling the smack to the junkies. They would look worse than ever, often toothless. Sometimes they would vaguely recognise me and ask me for gear but I'd quickly insist they had mistaken me for someone else and tell them to "fuck off".

In the Penthouse or the Towers pub I had a little bit of street cred. Lots of people knew that I had been knocking around with Marlo Hyland and that gave me a bit of respect. I never spoke about it with anyone though; it would have been far too dangerous. By and large I had got myself off the coke. I would do it the odd time socially but it wasn't a big deal for me. For the first time I felt like a proper teenager. My friends were normal kids like me, not older gangsters, and they were all doing courses or apprenticeships or working. Ma tried to encourage me to find something to do. She knew there was no way I was going back to school but I had always liked cooking so she found me a FAS training course to become a commis chef. The training took place in Sherriff Street in the north inner city so I fell into a little routine of getting up early in the morning and getting the bus into the city centre. I loved the course and met loads of other people my own age who had all sorts of different experiences in life.

One of my pals from Ballymun was working in a factory where they made office chairs and when a vacancy came up he recommended me. I was earning more than 200 quid a week working there at night and during the day I was doing my training as a chef. I used to love handing Ma her few bob every week for my rent and going out for a bit of a blow out at the weekends with my pals. Ma tried to talk to me about what had gone on over at Brian's but I couldn't bear to tell her. She told me that she had called up a few times to try to bring me home but that I was never there. She said that Rita had spoken to her and insisted that I was fine and that all me and Brian were doing was collecting pallets, which is what she believed. Ma's life was hard enough without me laying all my problems on her so I made a conscious decision not to tell her about the bad stuff. What was done was done, I reasoned and it was all behind me. I told her there was no need to worry and that I had just had a silly row with Brian. I told her I was bored there anyway and wanted a change of direction in life. I'm sure she knew there was more to it but she was happy enough to accept my explanation and not ask too many questions.

Niamh had a better idea of what had been going on. Over the years she had tried to talk to me but I'd always pushed her away. She knew I didn't want to talk about it and seemed to be just delighted I was back home and away from Brian. Natalie, like Ma, was oblivious to what I had really been doing but she couldn't have been happier to have me back. We were always very close and she'd missed me when I was gone. Our friends weren't far off the same age so it was fun for us to have one another.

For a while Brian left me alone. Then all of a sudden he started showing up. He called to the house a few times when I was out. Ma told me she warned him to stay away from me but I knew he would have just laughed at her. One day when I was making my way home from my course he pulled in beside me and tried to talk to me but I wanted nothing to do with him. "C'mon The Lips, when are ye gonna get over it. C'mon back. We've loads to do. Look, I'm sorry." I just ignored him and walked on. He seemed almost pathetic and I felt a bit sorry for him but I was resolute that I wasn't going back to the hell of living with him and not knowing when he was going to explode. He'd show up for a few days in a row and make a bit of a pest of himself and then he would disappear again. He tried telling me that the children missed me and were crying every night. That did make me feel bad. I hoped Robyn and Conor didn't think I'd abandoned them and that someday they would understand that I just had to go. Sometimes I'd hear nothing from him for a few weeks. I'd be hoping that he'd given up on me for good when out of the blue he'd pop up again. It was very strange. I changed my phone a few times but he kept getting my number and ringing and texting me.

I'd been at home for about five months when all of a sudden he started to contact me in earnest. This time he was insistent that we meet. I told him I didn't want to know but he said there was a big problem and that things were about to get crazy. "The Lips, I'm tellin' ye. Things are getting bad. Ye need to talk to me. For yer own sake." I ignored him as best I could but I was curious. He told me he had bought me a motorbike for my 17th birthday and that it was sitting unused and gathering dust up at Mitchelstown Cottage. I didn't reply. He started calling to the house again but I'd stay upstairs and Ma or Niamh would deal with him. He texted about his big plans, saying that he just needed to make a bit more money and then he would be moving to the country. I'd heard it all before but I was older now and I knew there was no milk round for me and I'd never be getting the keys for Mitchelstown Cottage. There was something different about Brian but I couldn't put my finger on it.

Then one night I was lying upstairs on my bed. My phone beeped. It was Brian. "Fucking urgent," the text read. I wasn't going to answer it but I was curious. I sent him back a question mark. "The Big Fella is out for you. Need to meet. Not much time." I sat up in bed. He'd got my attention now. Nobody wanted to be on Marlo Hyland's radar, least of all me. "WTF?" I typed. "Thinks you're a rat. Wants to burn out your Ma. Knows you are there," he replied. A chill ran down my spine as I stared down at my phone. I was confused. There was no reason for Marlo Hyland to think I was a rat. I had never spoken to a soul about him or anything we'd done. But the truth isn't always currency in gangland and I knew that.

"WTF?" I typed again. "Need to meet ASAP," he wrote. "See you in 20." I put down my phone, my heart racing, and threw on a tracksuit and a pair of runners before slipping out the front door and waiting outside on the front wall. Brian pulled up in a beautiful new Audi and I got in. "What the fuck is goin' on?," I asked him but he drove straight towards Mitchelstown Cottage.

His behaviour was very strange but he started reciting where Niamh was working, where Natalie was attending college and what time my Ma's shift work was at. "Marlo knows it all," he said. "A copper told me he wants you whacked. He says he has a pipe bomb with your Ma's name on it." None of it made sense to me. "But why? What am I supposed to have done?" I said.

"Cops are all over him. He thinks there's a rat. He think you are de rat." I had a sinking sense of familiarity as I watched the houses and street signs go by on the drive to Mitchelstown Cottage. "I'll sort it for you The Lips. I'll square it. My guy is gonna keep his ear to the ground for ye. There's a few jobs to do and then we're done with them. We're done. The cops are all over him, all over the Bradleys. We'll go it on our own, The Lips. I've it all sorted. I've everything worked out. I'm moving to the country. I just need to make enough money." With that he put his foot on the accelerator and pumped up the volume. Van Morrison came screaming out of the speakers: "*When there's no one complaining…..There'll be days like this.*"

CHAPTER 8

Everything had changed at Mitchelstown Cottage. As we pulled up the drive I couldn't help but notice the huge 14-foot wall that now separated the house from the shed. There were new windows, new cars in the drive and CCTV cameras all over the house. They seemed to be covering every inch of the grounds and it was clear there was some heightened security risk. "You sure it's me that Marlo's after?" I asked Brian sarcastically as the car ground to a halt on the pebbles. We got out and I walked ahead of Brian through the back door into the kitchen expecting to see Rita sitting in her usual chair smoking a cigarette. There were new units and a fancy granite worktop. There was a new couch and a new TV and the smell of stew cooking on the hob. "Hiya," a female voice said and all of a sudden I noticed a very attractive looking woman who I had never seen before standing beside the kitchen door . She was stunning with dark long hair down her back, large brown eyes and a body like a page 3 model.

CHAPTER 8

She was wearing skinny jeans and knee-high boots with a tight vest top barely covering her boobs.

"Where's Rita?" I asked her as I looked around expecting Robyn and Conor to come tearing towards me at any minute. The house was quiet except for the faint noise of a television set in the distance. Brian laughed behind me. "The Lips, meet Mandy. Mandy, meet the Lips." I stared at her and I must have looked her up and down because she threw her head back and smiled and gave me a little curtsey before walking over and attaching herself to Brian's arm. "I've heard all about ye, Joey," she said. "Brian does nothin' but talk about ye. Its lovely to meet ye." Brian grinned from ear to ear. "Rita's gone," he said.

I had so many questions but they would have to wait. Mandy fussed around the kitchen as Brian announced that we were all going to sit down for a meal. I was really confused and was trying to pinch myself to make sure I wasn't actually asleep and dreaming it all. In lots of his texts, even the most recent ones, Brian had insisted that Rita and the kids were missing me and were dying for me to come home. It seemed like they were gone in the refurbishments. Mandy brought the plates to the table and walked over to the door which led out into the hallway. She balanced on one shapely leg and leaned out the door. "Mondo. Mondo. Yer dinner." I had to stifle a laugh. Mondo was the name of the one of the characters in the TV soap *Fair City* and I had really never heard of anyone else with that name in my life. I was almost expecting the actor who played the character to walk in and for a camera crew to come behind him to film my reaction. Instead, a child of about 10 came in the door and sat down beside me. "Hi Joey," he said.

We exchanged pleasantries over the meal and I complimented Brian on the work he had done around the house while he asked me how my family was. "How's the auld slapper?" he said, referring to my Ma. Mandy and Mondo laughed but I just looked down into my plate. I hated it when Brian called Ma that. Once Mondo had finished his meal he went back to his room. Mandy sat for a while chatting but then she got up and pottered around cleaning up the dishes before disappearing off too. Then the real talk started. "She's a fuckin' roide. Isn't she?" Brian asked. I nodded in agreement. There was no doubt that Mandy was one of the best looking women I had ever laid eyes on and that Brian had hit the jackpot. She couldn't have been more different to Rita who was kind of conservative-looking in her own way. "Peter Joyce's sister," Brian said. "She was me cleaning lady but I had to let her give me a dustin' down." Brian roared, laughing at himself.

I had a vague recollection of a story about Peter Joyce's sister living with some mega big drug dealer in England but Brian was quick to fill in any gaps in my memory. He told me that Mandy had returned to Ireland earlier that year after a very "upsetting" incident in the UK. He said her partner was Mark Connor, a hugely wealthy heroin supplier who had three houses in the UK and lots of dosh. He had been linked to a Liverpudlian drug lord called Curtis Warren who was so wealthy he'd made it onto the *Sunday Times* rich list. Brian was almost salivating as he described the kind of money Connor had made and said he owned three houses and holiday homes abroad. The dream had ended with a bullet to the back of the head. Mandy had gathered up a few cheques that were lying around the house, Brian said, before being arrested and charged by the police with perverting the course of justice. She'd received a conditional discharge and returned to Ireland where Peter had tried to help get her back on her feet. He had encouraged Brian to take her on as a kind of cleaner or maid at Mitchelstown Cottage. The rest was history. "So when she arrived here with her duster I took one look at her and I thought wey hey hey," he said.

Brian told me he had realised that smack was the only game in town and he was a fool to be doing anything else. He said that Mandy smoked it but that she didn't have a habit – that she just enjoyed it every now and then. He said Mandy had helped him realise that the past was the past and he needed to move on. When it came to smack, he had decided, it was really just bad luck that he had been caught before. He told me that if he really wanted to make his fortune, smack – the 24/7 drug – was the only way to riches.

"It's the only way to hit the big time, The Lips. The market never shuts down. It's not like coke. The junkies want it all the time. They'll do anything to get it. It's like selling sweets to fuckin' children," he said.

Brian said he'd been busy while I was "off dossing" and had found a new supplier in Clondalkin who he called Tommo. He said he couldn't get enough smack to satisfy the customers he'd built up already and that he and Tommo were planning to take on Marlo for his north city turf. He said Tommo had been "handling matters" in his own area of Clondalkin and was soon going to be the biggest dealer in Dublin; Brian was to be his wing man.

I presumed he was talking about Thomas Hinchon. I'd heard about him being one of the big players in Clondalkin but had never met him. Brian said that working on his own for months had exhausted him and that he needed me back. He wasn't asking, he was telling me.

"What about Marlo?" I asked. I knew deep down that he'd lied about Marlo wanting to whack me and my Ma but I didn't trust him. He could have badmouthed me to someone so it would get back to Marlo. I'm sure they must have wondered why I was no longer around when Brian had never been without me before. He just brushed it off, insisting that he'd sort everything out but that I'd just have to do what he said. "Stick with me The Lips. Me and Tommo will sort out that problem."

CHAPTER 8

We stayed up talking until the early hours as he fantasised about moving to the country and leaving Mitchelstown Cottage to me. I was under no illusion at that stage but he was talking through his hat. It was the same old story he had spun since I was younger, but I was broken now and knew it was all a pipe dream. Eventually Brian told me to go to bed. He said he'd done up Robyn's old room for me and that I should get some sleep as we'd a busy day ahead. "Go wan up to your bedroom. It's all ready The Lips. All yer tings are there," he said. Just as I went to get up from the table he reached across, lifted my phone up and put it on the worktop. "I'll keep this. We need to be careful on the phones," he said. "I just want to text me Ma," I told Brian. "She'll be worried about me. I'll tell her I'm okay."

Brian stood over me as I typed out the message to Ma telling her that I wouldn't be coming home and that I had made up with Brian and was going to stay with him for a while. As I lay down for the night I knew my Ma would be totally gutted when she read the message. A text wasn't long enough to explain the real reason; that would be something that I would unravel much later with professional help. Back then I just knew I was trapped, shackled by my past, enslaved by the threat of a bullet or worse and I probably always would be. I'd been allowed my brief fling with freedom only because Brian had other things going on in his life. Whatever the truth about Rita, I was sure it wasn't as simple as Brian just deciding he wanted rid of her. I shuddered to think what she went through to get away from him. I wondered how the kids were and how she felt about being so quickly replaced. Sleep eventually came but there was a heaviness about it, a sense of dread. A darkness filtered into my dreams.

I woke to a phone ringing under my face and realised that Brian must have left it there during the night. I answered. It was a junkie looking for gear. "Hello, hello," the voice shrieked. "Can I meet ye? I have money." I was groggy but I knew how it worked and I told them to meet me in an hour near the Roadstone factory. I looked around. It had been dark when I had crawled into bed and I hadn't been able to find the light switch so I had just slept in my clothes. In the morning sun I could see the room properly. A huge wooden desk stood in the middle of it, complete with two sets of weighing scales. A slab of white sat on the right hand side and a slab of brown on the left. The table was spotlessly clean and was covered by pestles and mortars, teaspoons, tablespoons, bags, cling film, screwdrivers, a few scalpels and Sellotape. The walls were still covered in the *101 Dalmatians* sketches and *Rugrat* drawings chosen by Robyn when Billy had done up the room for her. The windows were skylights looking out over the fields at Kilshane and had no curtains or blinds. I had slept on a single bed and there was a small set of drawers beside it with a little lamp which wasn't working.

The phone rang again. More business. I heard Brian making his way up the stairs. "Good morning The Lips. You

decided to wake up; the phones are going 90," he said, chuck-
ing two more mobiles onto the bed.

Everything, but at the same time nothing, had changed and
before I had time to draw breath or consider what was happening, I was back on the hamster wheel that was life with Brian
Kenny. I knew how it all worked. There were two phones for
the smack and one for the coke. Brian told me not to make any
small deals. he coke was to be bagged in oner bags, quarters,
half ounces and ounces. The smack was in eights, quarters
and ounces, and anything less than 120 a deal wasn't worth the
petrol. The smack phone rang constantly, all day and all night.
The coke phone was also busy, but would only really get going
at the weekend. I'd meet the customers on the network of back
roads surrounding the cottage. I'd meet them near the airport,
in pub car parks, on the roadside and even in the fields. I felt
sorry for the junkies with their down-on-their-luck stories about
sick children, violent landlords or school uniforms to buy. They
looked like skeletons. I don't know how many times I'd end up
hugging them or listening to their woes only to have to tell them
that they still had to pay me or I'd get kicked around the place.
Sometimes I'd sub them a tenner and use my own money to
pay for their gear. But next time they'd be after even more help
so I had to harden up very quickly. Brian would go mad if he
ever heard that I'd been nice or if the junkies specifically asked
for me. "Ye need to toughen up, you stupid fuck. They'll eat ye
alive. Never, ever do anything for a dirty junkie."

Brian threw me a tenner a deal but every time I built up any cash, he took it from me and told me he'd look after it for me. He paid for everything, the food for the house, the petrol for the cars, the drinks when we were out. He hadn't bought me a bike for my birthday – that was another lie – but a few days after I returned, we went to a bike shop where I picked out a Honda CBR250. It was mainly to speed up my drug deliveries, but Brian made out like it was a big gift for me and I did see it that way too; I thought it was very generous. Brian bought me boxer shorts, socks, trousers, shirts and a few jumpers. I wore a tracksuit for work but whenever we went out, Brian would tell me to dress in cardigans and pants just like him.

Brian did all his business on the phones. He'd never change the number and never accept an order over text. Either he or I had to talk to the customer directly. We knew most of them already, unless the junkies had passed on their number to someone else. I was always nervous meeting first-time customers in case they were cops. The whole business had completely taken off since I'd been away and Brian was making serious money.

Very early on I was sent out to meet Tommo in Clondalkin. It was Thomas Hinchon all right. I went out on the motorbike and met him at the back of Neilstown. He told me to take off my leathers and strapped the smack to my body, Sellotaping it around my torso and legs before I got dressed again. I made the trip every couple of weeks; I would hand him around €30k in exchange for three bars measuring about 12 ounces each.

CHAPTER 8

It was much easier to get around on the bike . I could nip
through traffic and my helmet hid my identity. I'd bag the coke
when I got home.., I hid the cash and the drugs in a load of
metal flasks – the type you'd put soup or coffee in – and buried
them all around the house in the ditches. I bought a load of
Rubik's cubes and filled them with 8s. I could fit 10 into each
one, worth €2500, and I hid them in the pillars at the front of
the house so I could just grab one as I was leaving.

In my room I'd mix the coke with teething powder which
I'd buy in a load of different chemists to double each deal.
Sometimes I'd mix laundry detergent in as well, but not so
much it stank. This would bulk up the coke from one ounce
to two or three. Brian insisted we kept the drugs outside the
house as much as we could, particularly at the front or in the
fields outside his land so it'd be impossible to prove they were
his if he was raided. "Ye better not get me caught. Do ye hear
me? It'll be your fault if we get caught." When I look back I
realise I was the one taking all the risks, transporting the drugs
and selling them.

There were guns in the house which had never been there
before. There was a pump action shotgun in the bedroom
and Brian had taken to walking around the house with it.
He regularly came into my room with it in the middle of the
night. I couldn't understand why he was more paranoid about
being caught with drugs than with guns but there was no logic
to him at all. Brian would have made a great army sergeant if

he had put his mind to an honest career. He kept me awake all the time - sometimes I didn't know if it was day or night. I was constantly working and if I wasn't bagging and selling his drugs, I was cleaning up, washing the yard or painting the house. I never ever woke naturally.

It took me a while to realise that Brian was smoking heroin too. I had noticed a funny smell around the house coming from his bedroom. He had said that Mandy liked a bit of a smoke but the smell was constant and there was no way she could have produced that much on her own. Mandy didn't look like a junkie. I suppose she didn't have to go through the same hardships as the others to get her gear – she had just moved in with a drug dealer so she had a constant supply whenever she wanted it. She was clean enough and always fairly pleasant to me but she spent most of her time in the bedroom with Brian. I was surprised because Brian had always said that junkies were dirty and repulsed him. He was embarrassed that he was on the gear but he kept telling me he could take it or leave it and that he didn't have a problem with it.

In August 2002 Brian told me that he had to do a final job for the Big Fella but it really was the last. His police contacts had told him that Marlo and the Bradleys were red hot and there was all sorts of surveillance on them; but you never really knew whether to believe him or not. He said Detective Kevin Stratford was making a career out of bringing them down and he wouldn't stop until he had cleaned the place up. The

CHAPTER 8

target of this last job was a cash-in-transit van due to deliver money to an ATM machine at the Omni Shopping Centre in Santry. It was the usual routine, Wayne had been watching the van and timing its arrival and departure to precision; it was happening early in the day. They got ready as usual in the shed and when the Bradleys arrived they made a big deal about me being back. They were slagging Brian off and he didn't like it. I knew the Bradley brothers liked me and would have taken me from Brian if they had the chance. They had no idea how Brian treated me.

When they got back they were very excited and it was clear they had obtained a serious amount of cash. The minute they got back, Fatpuss phoned Marlo. "We've done it this time boss. We've hit the fuckin' jackpot," he told him. Fatpuss and Brian looked like two children as they reached their hands into the bags and threw armfuls of money up over their heads and out onto the shed floor. When Wayne arrived he joined in. They were so excited that I thought Brian was going to explode. When they had their fun, they went into the kitchen and told me to pick up all the money and bring it to the table for counting. It took me about an hour to pick it all up and it took them another two hours to count it all. There were 50s, 20s, 10s and even 5s but as the piles got higher and higher it was clear that this was their biggest ever robbery. By the time the money was counted there was a little more than €400k, more cash than I had ever seen in my life. Brian was almost drooling but his face reddened as he was handed €50k. "We are getting the same but Marlo gets the rest," they said. "It was his job." Then they left. There were no celebrations, no renditions of "Days Like This". And I knew that he meant it when he said he wouldn't do any more jobs with them. He disappeared into the bedroom with Mandy and it wasn't long before the familiar sweet smell of smack began to waft along the corridors of Mitchelstown Cottage.

I was deeply uncomfortable about the fallout with Marlo and the Bradleys. I didn't know whether the claims Brian made about Marlo being after me were true. It certainly didn't look like there was any problem when I'd seen the Bradleys, and it was becoming more and more likely that he had made it all up in order to get me back. I knew Brian had decided he'd outgrown them and become too big for them but I also knew he wasn't diplomatic enough to cut ties and move away from them in a controlled manner. After the Omni job he stopped taking their calls and even delighted in telling me that he'd refused to talk to Marlo. Fatpuss called at the house a few weeks later and he left him standing in the yard. As far as he was concerned, Tommo was the only supplier in town and Brian was going to leave the others in the dust.

Hinchon ran a big mob in Clondalkin and Brian told me was dealing with a big supplier from Kildare who had once been linked with John Gilligan, his criminal hero. He was much younger than Brian but extremely violent and he had a young lad working for him like me who seemed to do most of the hard labour. Hinchon was seriously ambitious and Brian said he wanted to take over Ballymun and Finglas. He had problems on his own patch but he was dealing with them bit by bit. The stakes were much higher than when Brian was delivering drugs on his milk float but he seemed to revel in the increased danger. He had become obsessed with Tony Soprano and watched back-to-back episodes of the show whenever he sat down in front of the TV. It was like he thought he was him.

Within weeks of the Omni robbery, three men claiming to be IRA visited the house saying they knew Brian was dealing drugs and wanting a cut. He told them they weren't getting a penny and pulled a gun on them at which point they left. Then a few weeks later I was asleep one night when I was woken by a commotion downstairs. I heard the front window smashing and then Brian roaring, "I have a gun." I ran downstairs and saw three guys climbing through the window. Brian was standing in the darkness and Mandy had come out of the bedroom. The kid Mondo made his way out of his room and started screaming so I just grabbed him and dragged him upstairs with me. I opened the attic window and pushed him out ahead of me and then joined him on the roof. We crouched down and I tried to comfort him. I didn't know whether it was the police or the IRA, but then I saw Brian running out into the back yard with three masked men after him. They were all running around in circles and then the gunshots started. In the panic I saw Brian fall to the ground before the men then tried and failed to pull open the gate at the back. They were trapped in the yard and getting frantic. They pulled and pulled at the gate but it had been broken for years and had been wedged shut with a spoon. I shouted down at them to pull the spoon out of the lock and ducked my head, not knowing whether they would shoot up at me or not. But it seemed they just wanted to get out of there and I watched them disappear down the driveway.

There were faint whimpers coming from Brian and I knew he was injured. I leapt back into the bedroom and took the stairs in one bound as I raced out to the yard. Mandy was on the phone calling for an ambulance and I knelt down beside Brian. He was breathing but there was blood everywhere and his eyes were rolling back in his head. "Stay wit me, Brian. I'm getting help," I begged him. He whispered to me that he wanted to ring Rita and speak to Conor but he was in no fit state. "Clean up," he managed to spit out, and I suddenly realised I had to get all the stuff out of the house before the police arrived. I told Mandy to stay with him and to keep talking to him. I raced back into the house, grabbed the guns and the smack and sprinted back out towards the fields at the back of the house where I dumped the lot in a ditch on our neighbour's land. I can remember very logically asking myself why there were so many guns and what the hell Brian was doing with them. I ran back to the house, grabbed the phones and stuffed them under my bed. I threw a blanket over the rest of the stuff on the table, hoping the Gardai wouldn't look upstairs when they arrived. After what seemed like an eternity the ambulance came, followed closely by two Garda cars. The paramedics strapped Brian onto a stretcher and Mandy went with him to the hospital. I could see that his back was all bloody.

Two of the Gardai stayed behind and asked me what had happened but I told them I hadn't seen anything. I said I'd woken up to a bit of noise and found Brian in the yard. They stayed in the kitchen and just went to look at the broken window at the front. I didn't hear anything for hours and hours but eventually Billy arrived. He told me that Brian was going to be okay but he needed an operation on his back to remove the bullets. Mandy had told him I'd saved Brian's life and he said he was very grateful. After a few days I went to see him in hospital. He was sitting up in silk pyjamas with some of his family. He was very emotional. "You saved my life The Lips. I love you like a son, you know that." I sat on the side of his bed while visitors came and went and eventually just the two of us were left. Suddenly his mood changed. "What the fuck did you do with the gear?" he asked me. "Where's the fuckin' guns." His eyes were bulging out of his head. I told him I had dumped them up the fields and hadn't gone near them since. "Did ye wrap them? Did ye wrap the smack?" I told him I didn't have time ; the guns would be okay but the drugs would probably be wet. "Ye stupid cunt," he hissed.

I'd ignored the phones for a few days, terrified that the cops would be crawling all over Mitchelstown Cottage. When it became clear they weren't coming back, I went out and found the smack and the coke. Some of it was sodden and had to be flushed down the toilet, but I salvaged what I could and got things up and running again. By the time he got home it was business as usual but Brian was in a bad way. He had a hole in his back which you could have put your fist through and he needed help to go to the toilet, to dress and to change his bandages. He stayed in his bedroom most of the time shouting orders from his bed. The waft of heroin was constant and his paranoia was at a new level.

Sometimes anything I did was wrong and even when I'd be helping him off the toilet and wiping his ass, he'd be telling me I was disrespecting him, looking at him wrong or sneering at him. It didn't take him long to get enough energy back to wallop me whenever he could. Mandy made him soup and stews and lay beside him in bed as he smoked his heroin. It took at least two months for the hole to heal a bit but he never seemed to realise how lucky he was that the bullet missed his spine. Hinchon came to visit and they talked business in the bedroom. I was keeping the show on the road but I could tell that Brian was frustrated that he couldn't be more hands on.

Whether it was the brush with death or pressures from his family, Brian decided that he was going to get married once he got better. His ma was delighted and she booked a church in Drogheda for February 21 2003 and a reception at the Morning Star pub nearby for the occasion. I had turned 18 a few weeks previously and despite being fed drink and coke for five years, the wedding toast was the legal drink Brian Kenny had bought for me. Mandy wore white and Brian's brother was the Best Man while I was a groomsman. There were Limos and Rolls Royces, champagne and all the trappings and the party went on until late into the night. But afterwards it was straight back to business and Brian and Mandy didn't even take a honeymoon. The truth was that he was married to smack and to all the money that came with it.

The rest of that year became more and more chaotic. I was taking a huge amount of cocaine: anything he was giving me and whatever else I could get my hands on. I had to start wearing gloves while bagging the drugs because if I put my hands to my face, my lips were numb for hours after and I was getting lots of infections. The more coke I was on the less pain I felt and the more energy I had and I operated like a robot, running the business. Brian had obviously started shooting up heroin soon after he got shot, and he was off his head all the time. Sometimes he'd fall asleep at the wheel and if he wore T-shirts I could see the holes up his arms. If he left the door open I could see that his bedroom was covered in tinfoil and needles. But the money was still flowing in. I just kept collecting it, counting it and burying it in the fields and ditches around the house. I hadn't seen Auld Fella John in years and I don't really know what Brian thought he was going to do with all this money but even in his drug haze he was obsessed with it. He knew where every Euro was and how many were in each flask. He was far more violent than ever before. He broke nearly all of the pool cues over my back in anger; he would change in an instant from being friendly to accusing me of laughing at him. He pointed guns at me all the time, locked me out of the house at night in the cold and wet and would often wake me up with his hands around my neck.

Brian had odd ideas about things. I remember the night when I had first arrived back, we stayed up and talked about Mandy and his plans. He told me that she hadn't come to him-empty handed but had "brought something to the table". He meant by this that she had some money, and he had sold a convertible car which she had brought from England. He was just so obsessed with money. But he was also of the opinion that now Mandy was his wife, she should start acting like one, and that meant he had to get her off the heroin. He discovered some place in England where you could have surgical implants put in which would reject the heroin. It sounded a bit like the thing that George Best had implanted in his stomach for the alcohol. It was expensive but he convinced Mandy that the two of them needed to go over and get it done and get themselves off the smack. They booked in and I was left in the house to mind Mondo and run the business.

They were supposed to be gone for five days or so but the day after they left Brian called me to ask me to collect him at Dublin Airport; he was coming back to make sure everything was going okay. I wondered what had happened but did as I was told and picked him up at the agreed time. In the car he told me that Mandy had gone ahead with the operation but he hadn't needed it after all as he didn't have a problem with heroin. He said he had been on methadone for the few days he was in England but hadn't needed it in the same way she did.

"I'm not an addict, The Lips. I can take it or leave it whenever I want," he said. He was very emotional. As I was driving he put his hand on mine and told me that he was really proud of me and that we wouldn't be where we were without my hard work. He said when Mandy came back and was sorted out, he'd be able to do more and we just needed to give it all one final push before he'd be able to move up country.

As soon as we got home to Mitchelstown Cottage his attitude changed. There were unwashed dishes in the sink which me and Mondo had used for our breakfast and the place was a little untidy. He completely lost it and started ranting and raving at me and Mondo, telling us we couldn't be trusted on our own and that he couldn't even go away for a day. He turned on Mondo and tore through a cupboard looking for a bowl. "Ye need to be fuckin' fed? I'll feed ye." He picked up a bag of dog food and poured it into the bowl. "Eat tha', ye little fuck." Mondo looked shocked but Brian caught him by the back of the head and shoved his face into the bowl. "Eat, ye cunt, eat" he shouted. He trashed around the house and walloped me around the head before storming into his bedroom and slamming the door. Within minutes there was the sound of tinfoil and the sweet smell of heroin wafting through the house.

For three or four days Brian stayed in his room shooting up while myself and Mondo walked on eggshells around the house. Eventually he told me he was going back to get Mandy and I dropped him at the airport again. He was in good form. "Maybe I'll get a proper wife back and not some junkie," he said as he waved goodbye to me. The implant surgery had been a success but at the first opportunity when Mandy got back to Mitchelstown, she whispered to me to go out to the fields and get her some coke. I could see she was desperate for something and the heroin wasn't going to work. I felt sorry for her so I went out and grabbed some for her but I made sure to mix more powder in it so that if Brian weighed it, it wouldn't look as if it had been nicked. Despite being strung out he knew exactly how many ounces he had buried in those fields.

While tensions were frayed at Mitchelstown Cottage, the year 2003 was a heady one throughout the city and gangs were going to war like never before for control of drug turf. Gangland was becoming more and more dangerous and it was a constant struggle for survival of the fittest. In my old neighbourhood of Blanchardstown a drug war was raging.

The Westies who had for years ruled the territory with an iron fist had imploded, dividing into murderous rivalry between Sugg and Coates and their former pals Andrew and Mark Glennon. In August 2003 Bernard Verb Sugg, Stephen's brother, was murdered while he sat in a pub having a pint. Everyone knew the Glennons had done it but Sugg was the 16th gangland murder victim in Ireland that year. Still buoyed up with ambition and cocaine, Sugg and Coates had moved to Spain in order to establish themselves as a mob on the Costa, but within the year they had gone missing without a trace.

In Crumlin and Drimnagh another young gang had split, forcing former friends into deadly rivalry. By the time their war was over, 18 people would be dead. In Finglas Marlo was coming under more and more pressure not only from the Gardai who had launched Operation Anvil to take his mob down, but also from internal rivalries as one of his underlings was beginning to make moves against the boss.

Closer to home for us, Hinchon and his mob were at war with another group in Clondalkin. It was rumoured that his associates had been behind the murder back in December 2001 of a 22-year-old guy called Simon Doyle who had been shot outside his mother's house. An older criminal, Maurice Bo Bo Ward, had been killed in retaliation for Doyle's killing but I don't think he had anything to do with it. Throughout the year Brian's relationship with Hinchon had intensified and they became almost inseparable. Brian had effectively become one of his henchmen. He was no longer just buying drugs off him but was involving himself in Hinchon's disputes and beating people up on his behalf. That same desire to be part of something big that had led to him becoming engulfed by Marlo and the Bradleys had now been transferred to Hinchon. Brian would literally have done anything for him. Hinchon became a regular visitor to Mitchelstown Cottage and in order to curry favour, Brian allowed him to use his shed to store anything he wanted. He would come to stay saying there was a warrant out for him and he needed to lie low for a while. Invariably a group of his crew would join him and we'd end up partying in the shed for days on end. Everyone knew that Hinchon was a millionaire and having boxed off all of west Dublin; he now set his sights on north Dublin. His crew were showing up at the house all the time and the amount of stuff being stored in the shed meant there was no room for much else. But Brian wanted to be the golden boy and bought a container near Ashbourne so he could keep more stuff for them. Van loads of cigarettes, clothes, alcohol, cars and even pub fruit were constantly arriving.

At one point during the year Hinchon was locked up but was out after a few months and a huge party was held at Mitchelstown to celebrate. I remember one night when he'd stayed at the house he called me into his room in the morning and asked me why I was always covered in bruises and cuts. I told him I was just clumsy and needed to be a bit more careful of myself. I think he knew that Brian was beating me and he told me that if I ever wanted to, I could work directly for him in Clondalkin where he would put me up in a new apartment. "I mean it. Ye can come work for me whenever ye want, kid. I'll look after ye." I told him I was happy where I was. Brian had been listening at the door the whole time and as soon as Hinchon left he started attacking me, telling me I had to stay loyal to him. Even though he heard me refuse the offer, he still beat me so badly with a baseball bat that I couldn't walk for days. I couldn't even deliver the drugs and he had to do the drops himself.

I knew that everything had gone up a gear when Brian told me that we were going to move a jeep for Hinchon, bring it back to Mitchelstown Cottage, and dismantle it in the shed. He told me the jeep was packed with heroin and was being delivered straight from the UK. He was very excited to be involved at such a high level of Hinchon's operation but I knew that I'd do big jail time if I got caught with it. I was very nervous but before we set off for Clondalkin he gave me two huge lines of coke. The jeep was parked up in Neilstown and when we arrived, Hinchon and one of his sidekicks were sitting in a top-of-the-range BMW nearby. Brian got in with them and I was given the key for the jeep. I walked past it to make sure it was working and when I heard the beep of the locks, I hopped in, started it up and put my foot to the floor.

I booted off towards Lucan leaving the lads behind me in the BMW. I got out onto the motorway and drove full throttle across the M50. My plan was simple, I was stopping for no one. The phone rang and I answered it on speaker. Brian was showing off with the others in the car. "Fuck me, The Lips. Slow down. We can't even see ye." There were roars of laughter. "Ring Mandy when you are nearby and she'll open the gates." I was sweating inside the gloves and my nose was dripping as I sped onwards towards the airport and then back around to Kilshane Cross where I rang Mandy and told her I was coming in to land.

I handbraked straight through the shed doors and jumped out of the jeep throwing my gloves into the stove out the back. The lads arrived a good 10 minutes later, with Hinchon congratulating Brian on my driving. They all started smoking smack while me and Brian got our overalls on and started dismantling the jeep. I couldn't believe the amount of drugs that were in it, easily half a million Euros' worth. When we got it all out, Hinchon told Brian to hold a kilo back for himself and me. Brian was happy - €40k worth of smack for an hour's work. "Easy money, The Lips, easy money," he shouted when the lads left.

He still had the boat and the jet skis up at Clogherhead and would sometimes take day trips on it but Brian always wanted more. He wanted a bigger boat and a mobile home there too so we could all spend weekends together. This time, the "we" was me, him, Mandy and Mondo. He had plenty of money to buy a caravan but buying just wasn't in his remit.

CHAPTER 8

Instead Hinchon came over one night and they headed out to Bray to have a look around the boatyard. Brian saw what he wanted, burned the locks off the yard gates, connected a boat to his car and drove it back to the house. Then he went back for the jet skis. But the night was still young as far as the lads were concerned and they had spotted a new caravan in one of the houses in the town, so they went back out and stole it. Brian parked it up in the front garden and brought the new boat up to Clogherhead. Stealing was just as much a drug for them as crack. They were more minted than they could ever have dreamed of but they were still compelled to steal. It was in their blood; they felt that the rest of the world owed them and they were taking what was rightfully theirs.

To make things even more chaotic I received some news earlier that year that shocked and thrilled me in equal measure. A girl I had been seeing on and off since I went back in Ballymun for those few months with my friends had phoned me one day to tell me she was pregnant. The baby was mine, she said. I was stunned and I didn't know what to do but I told her that I was thrilled and would help out whatever way I could. She had no idea of the situation I was in or that I was dealing drugs. I kept the news to myself because I knew Brian wouldn't take it well but I had eventually confided in Mandy. Instead of helping me she went straight to him and told him. Brian hit the roof and told me that I wasn't to have any contact with her and that a baby would ruin my life. "She's only looking for fuckin' money. Tell her it's not yours and even if it is ye want nothing to do with it."

I tried to stay in touch with her a bit but whenever Brian found out he battered me and I was afraid he was going to start threatening her. He told me she was only after his money and that I wasn't to let on where I lived or anything.

The baby was born in January 2004 and a friend phoned to tell me that it was a little girl. I had a daughter and I was dying to go and see her but Brian refused to allow me. I begged and begged him. He eventually took me to a lockup where he was storing a container of baby clothes which he had nicked. He let me pick out one outfit and drove me up to the girl's mother's. He waited in the car while I handed the little dress in at the door. I'm sure they thought I was the worst person in the world but I couldn't tell them and I genuinely feared for their safety if I pushed it any further. For the meantime the best I could do for my child was to stay away.

Hinchon and his mob's comings and goings were becoming more and more frequent and I gathered from the conversations that things were heating up out in Clondalkin. Brian seemed to have got himself involved in every aspect of Hinchon's business, even down to beating up small time junkies that had annoyed him. I remember him proudly telling me about one girl who used to pay when she got her children's allowance but who had tried to get away with it one week. Brian had gone personally to collect the money from her and when she came out of the welfare office and took off running, he chased her and dragged her by the hair to the ground, kicking and punching her until he got the money from her. "Ye should have seen her, the slut. Squealing away on the ground. It was gas. Tommo laughed his head off at her," he boasted.

Hinchon was certainly trying to gain ground and to acquire a reputation for himself as the biggest and the best. Brian was adamant that he would be at his side to face down any threat to that dream. I was deeply uncomfortable with it all. I had to admit that I had always quite liked the Bradleys and some of the guys from Finglas, but the Hinchon crew were different. They were in a completely different league and I wanted nothing to do with them if I could at all avoid it. With Brian's business so busy ,I was working flat out keeping the money coming in. This suited both Brian and me as it prevented me getting dragged into Hinchon's wars.

On what was otherwise a normal day in April 2004 I was upstairs in my room bagging up smack and counting and rolling wads of money, when I saw Hinchon arriving on a green Kawasaki motorbike. After a short while he drove off again, this time with Brian on the back. The two of them were dressed from head to toe in black leathers and Brian was just closing his visor as they made their way out the gate. They looked like they were on a mission.

At some point in the early evening I heard a car flying up the drive and minutes later Mandy called me to come down. I hadn't reached the back door when I could hear Brian shouting in the shed. Something serious had gone down.

From the yard I could smell the turpentine and hear the frantic chatter of Brian and Hinchon. I put my head around the door to see the two of them stripped and washing themselves in paintbrush cleaner and petrol. Brian handed me two heavy black bin bags and took a meat cleaver from a wall. "Cut them up and fuckin' burn them. NOW!" I took the bags. Inside were the leather jackets and trousers they had been wearing earlier in the day when they left on Hinchon's bike. I ran out the back of the shed to the pot-bellied stove. I had burned balaclavas and gloves in it for years but the leather emitted little more than big heavy billows of black smoke. Brian eventually came out and told me to put them in the boot of the car. Then he called me back into the shed.

The moment he handed me the gun I knew someone was dead. My heart started to race and I moved like a robot. I felt the weapon cold in my hand as I raced across the fields. I tore at the grass, pulling tufts of it back. I was gasping for breath by the time I pushed open the kitchen door. The sweet smell of smack filled the air and Brian and Hinchon were at the table smoking. Brian looked up at me. "We're after shootin' a fella. I'm after doing it once, I've no problem doin' it again. Open your mouth and I'll kill you and your fuckin' family." My blood ran cold.

CHAPTER 9

I was barely able to press the buttons on the remote control as I desperately looked for news of the shooting. The smell of the smack and petrol was making me feel nauseous, my knees were buckling and my hands were shaking like crazy. In the kitchen there was pandemonium. "What if he isn't fuckin' dead?" I heard Brian shout. "We're absolutely fucked," replied Hinchon.

From Brian's bedroom I could hear them pacing, sucking and sniffing. They were getting very agitated and repeatedly trying to ring "Robbie" and "Richie". The headlines were confusing. There had been a shooting outside Cloverhill Prison. Someone was injured. Later it said on teletext on another channel that, "A man has died after being shot…" "He's after dyin'," I shouted into the kitchen. There were whoops and shouts of jubilation. My stomach lurched and it was all I could do to swallow the vomit in my mouth.

The next few hours are still frames in my memory as if I was watching on from a distance: the chinking glasses, the lines of coke, the high fives. "He was a big fella," Brian kept repeating. "He jumped around as I pumped him." He'd make his body wobble like a fish and Hinchon would collapse into laughter. "This is my playground now, Kenny… All mine, ha, ha, ha, ha." I tried to stay quiet, to disappear into the ground but every so often they'd look over and turn their attention to me. "I've done it once. I've no problem doing it again, The Lips. I'll do yer family too."

My head raced. Brian had done some bad things but murdering another human being was so far outside my moral code that I couldn't even process it. Through their drug haze they noticed my distress. "Sit down there, The Lips," Brian said. His eyes were wild. "Me and Thomas trust you. You know we do. I know you won't say anything because… Well you know that I would happily blow your fuckin' head off, don't you?" I could smell the whiskey on his breath and see the track marks up his arms. They both smiled; Hinchon then slammed his fist down on the table and told me that if I ever breathed a word he wouldn't rest until me, my family and my baby daughter were all in their graves. I nodded and heard myself promise them that I would never open my mouth.

When they left I went up to my bedroom and stared at the wall. Time passed. I didn't move. I didn't think. I just lay there. When Brian came back he called up for me to come out to the shed. I knew what was coming. He put a gun in my mouth; the cold of the metal tasted bitter and he pushed it so far to the back of my throat that I gagged. He undid his trousers. I shut my eyes. I thought of the young man he had killed. The news said he was only 25 – just a few years older than me.

Later he made me stand in the field while he shot at me, to the left and to the right. I willed my legs to hold me still. The bullets moved past me like a breeze. His words were crisp and clear. "You're small, The Lips. Easy to bury."

In the days that followed I resigned myself to death. He came with me on the drug drops and watched me all the time. He was with me upstairs, he was beside me in the kitchen. He carried a pump action shotgun around and pointed it at me all the time, laughing manically when I'd beg him not to kill me. He'd make me read out the news stories to him. The poor guy he had killed was called Jonathan O'Reilly. He'd a young baby too, just like me. There was no picture of him but I couldn't get the image from the news reports out of my head, of the car covered in tarpaulin, hiding Brian's gruesome handiwork. I couldn't imagine how his family were coping, how his ma would feel. I knew I'd be dead soon too but my end wouldn't appear on news reports. Mine would be hidden away somewhere in the prison that was Mitchelstown Cottage and I'd rot in the fields amidst the flasks of money and smack.

At some point we collected the bike they had used for the murder from a house in Clondalkin. Brian drove it back and I followed in the car. He sent me off to burn the helmets and the leathers and the gloves. I took them to a place near the airport and as soon as it was done I came back immediately. Sometimes I'd go out on my own and return to find him standing in the yard with a stopwatch. "Where the fuck were ye?" he'd say as I'd pull in. I tried to go up to Ma's one day and I was stopped at a checkpoint. I'd no insurance or tax on the car so I ran like hell but was stopped by Gardai. I phoned and asked him to come and get me. He walloped me again and again when we got home, as if my head was a tennis ball. "I told ye not to go to yer Ma's. What did I fuckin' tell ye?"

I tried to do as I was told but the beatings carried on regardless. If I'd pulled in to get petrol I'd return to find him pacing the yard. "Where the fuck were ye?" he'd roar before I could explain. One night he beat me mercilessly with a sewer rod until I ran down the driveway, giving myself a shock on the gates as I climbed them. I dropped down onto the main road and tried to run, but he came out after me in his car and ran me off the road into a ditch. Then he picked me up and dragged me back to Mitchelstown Cottage where he raped me again in the privacy of the shed.

For days after this I couldn't get out of bed, I couldn't piss. He sent Mandy up to give me coke and he made the drug drops himself. If I slept I'd wake to find him whispering into my ear; "Imagine Mary's face when I turn up at her front door to blow her fuckin' head off. Think of Louise getting pulled over in her car with a boot load of heroin. You know why you have to keep your fuckin' mouth shut, don't you?"

CHAPTER 9

I had completely given up mentally. Fear engulfed me. Hinchon was in and out of Mitchelstown Cottage all the time. He came with news that Robbie O'Hanlon had been taken in for questioning but had kept his mouth shut. He seemed to have been one of Jonathan O'Reilly's guys but had clearly double-crossed him. They started to relax and joked about how easy it all was. I heard Brian asking Hinchon whether he was going to honour his side of the bargain. Hinchon said he would. I knew what that meant.

One night they got me out of bed to go with them in the car. They had a gun and two balaclavas and a flashlight. We headed for Meath where Fatpuss had just bought a house. They had the ingredients for a petrol bomb and they wanted me to crawl as close as I could to the garden and throw it at his car. When he came out, Brian was going to run over and shoot him. They dropped me off but I couldn't do what they said. When they, rang I lied and I told them I'd heard a police car so they aborted the mission and decided to try again another time.

That night sparked something in me, an awakening, a sense of survival which I thought was gone. I knew there was absolutely no way that I could take a life, or be at all involved in doing so. To me Jonathan O'Reilly's murder was so senseless, so wrong that it went against every beat of my heart. It sickened me beyond anything I could have ever imagined. I knew I had to get out. I had to get help. I had to tell someone what they had done. It was time to go home but escape wasn't going to be easy.

I started to really think about Mitchelstown Cottage and its surroundings. It really was like a prison with a big wall at the back. The gates were locked and there were security lights everywhere. But the other side of the cottage, the front, was never used and besides Mondo's bedroom, the front door and porch could provide possible escape routes. For days I hunted for the spare key every second I got and eventually found it in a drawer in the kitchen. One evening while Brian was out and Mandy was lying in bed I turned the lock and quickly put the latch on the outer door, closing them both behind me. I was soaking with sweat by the time I got back to my bedroom. For another two days I carried on as normal but every chance I got I'd check the doors were still open and that nobody had noticed they were unlocked. I knew exactly what I had to do. I just needed to wait for my chance.

And then one night there was a gap. Through the chink of the door into Brian's bedroom I could see he was out cold. Both he and Mandy were sleeping deeply, surrounded by needles and heroin. The big pump action shotgun lay on the ground next to him. I tiptoed upstairs and picked up the smack phone. I punched in Louise's number. She answered and I told her not to say anything but I needed her help. I needed her to listen and do exactly what I said. "Just ring once and hang up when you get here," I told her and then I waited.

My breath was short and my mouth was dry. My head was racing and my eyes darted around the room. The spiral

CHAPTER 9

stairs to the attic were painted red. They creaked like mad and Brian was a very light sleeper no matter how much drink and drugs he had taken. I waited with the phone. I thought about Jonathan O'Reilly and his family and the trauma his violent death must have caused. I thought about Hinchon and Brian laughing at him, about the fear that must have been etched on his face as he stared into the barrel of the gun, and the way they said he tried to escape. I heard creaks I had never heard before in that house. I heard my heart thundering in my chest.

And then it rang, just once, and I knew Louise, my brave sister, was outside and all I had to do was get to her. I contorted myself as I picked over the stairs and tiptoed to the front door hoping that I hadn't been rumbled. Just as I put my hand on the lock, I heard a voice behind me. "Joey. Where you going?" I turned to see Mondo standing in his pyjamas and looking like he was about to burst out crying. "Oh kid. Don't worry. I have to go out but you go back to bed," I whispered, ushering him to his room. "Everything is going to be okay. You go back to sleep." He looked unconvinced but I moved quickly. I opened the door, gently closed it behind me, then opened the outside porch door. As soon as I felt fresh air I ran faster than I had ever run before in my life, faster than I had that first night on the milk float, keeping right and low to avoid the security lights. I could see Louise's car at the gate. She had done just as I had asked her and killed her lights but kept her engine running. I ran and ran towards her, scaling the wall and jumping into the passenger seat of her Suzuki Swift. Louise didn't even ask a question but just floored the little car and we took off away from Mitchelstown Cottage and towards Finglas.

I was so glad to see her and I was relieved and terrified all in one go. "Louise. They killed that fella. They murdered him and they're going to murder me." I was frantic but Louise's military training kicked in and she stayed calm as she handed me her phone. "We need to ring Ma," she said. "She'll know what to do."

We picked Ma up in a car park and I collapsed into her arms. Through gasps and tears and palpitations I told them both what had happened. Ma told me everything was going to be alright but we had to go to the Gardai. I was terrified all over again. Brian had always said he knew the Gardai, I had heard him talking to them and I didn't think I could trust them. In the middle of it, Louise's phone rang. Brian was at Ma's house with a can of petrol and a lighter, ranting and raving. My brother John Paul and some of his friends had been there and frightened him off. I knew Mondo must have woken him up the minute I left. I had been lucky so far.

"I know a Garda in Ballymun," Ma announced. "We can trust him. He is a good man. He was good to me when you were all small. We can tell him. Jonathan's family deserves the truth." Everything Ma said was so right, so true, so pure. Her words were like a waterfall washing me clean, making me feel human again. Ma rang the Garda station and told them who she was and that she needed to get an urgent message to

Garda Stephen Daly about a murder. We drove around for hours until her phone eventually rang. Stephen was waiting for us at Ballymun station.

We must have looked a state, particularly me as we bundled in. Ma told Stephen what I had told her about Jonathan's murder and about Brian Kenny and Thomas Hinchon; she told them about the gun and the motorbike and said I wanted to tell them everything. I was put into a cell for my own safety while officers were rounded up from Lucan where the investigation into Jonathan's murder had hit a brick wall. My phone rang constantly and texts came one after the other from Brian. The Gardai told me to leave the phone and let him incriminate himself on it. "I want me fuckin' gun, get back to the house now" one read. More came, threatening to shoot me, Ma, Louise and even my baby daughter.

Ma stayed with me all the time holding my hand and encouraging me to do the right thing. At about 2am a man in uniform walked into the cell. He introduced himself as Detective Inspector Toddy O'Loughlin and I liked him the minute he shook my hand. He had a goodness in his eyes and he was very respectful to Ma.

I told him all about what had happened and how Brian and Hinchon had come back to the house and given me the gun. He told me he knew both of them but couldn't believe Kenny was involved in the O'Reilly murder because it was so far off his turf. I explained how he was buying his supplies off Hinchon and had started knocking around with him all the time. I told him how I suspected that they had agreed to help one another get rid of a mutual problem. He asked me a few times how old I was. I told him I was 19 but I must have seemed much younger.

Toddy explained to me that he needed to take a statement so he could obtain a warrant to search Mitchelstown Cottage. With Ma by my side I felt like I had a bit of strength but I also knew there was no turning back now. I had committed the ultimate sin of gangland – I had become a rat, and in so doing had spectacularly earned my nick name of Joey The Lips. All this time Toddy was ringing different people and getting them up out of bed. Detectives started arriving and lots of them popped their head into the room, no doubt curious to see this young lad who was signing his life away.

By 6am the warrant was ready and Toddy brought me and Ma out the back of the station to go with him to Mitchelstown Cottage. The reality of what I had done only hit me as we stepped out into the yard. It was early in the morning but it was May, and I blinked in the morning sun. Around 30 armed Gardai were gearing up for the raid. There were vans, battering rams, dogs, officers in body armour and specialist emergency response vehicles. It was surreal. Before Toddy gave the order to head to Mitchelstown he informed the troops that he had information there were guns in the house and he told them where they were stored. I lowered my eyes. Nobody likes a rat.

As we drove up to the house I could see van loads of officers surrounding Mitchelstown Cottage. I knew Brian was inside and I knew he was capable of shooting at anyone. We parked up on the opposite side. I closed my eyes and started to pray. When I opened them I saw two officers arrive at the gates with Brian between them, his hands over his head. They put him in the back of a car and minutes later I heard Mandy screaming as she was dragged away. Brian's father Billy was next on the scene and he seemed to leave quickly with Mondo. It was quick and efficient in the end but for me it was only the beginning.

It was decided that Ma would head home and get some rest as I joined the Gardai for the search. Exhausted, I walked Toddy and his men around the house showing them where everything was: the guns, the cash and the drugs. Upstairs in my room I showed them the table, the scales, the bags and the money yet to be counted and rolled. I pointed out the phones, the ones for the smack and the one for the coke. One of the officers looked at me and then all round the room. "Did you actually live here? Like this?" he asked. I looked at the tiny bed with the thin mattress, the broken lamp and the bare floorboards. I could see the officers looking at me in a funny way. "Where's your stuff?" another asked. "I don't really have anything," I said, feeling all of a sudden very vulnerable.

The pump action shotgun was on the floor of the kitchen where Brian had eventually dropped it after initially refusing to surrender to the Gardai. I showed them where he'd kept the ammunition and they found all his jewellery, his big gangster chains and more cash and mobile phones in his bedroom. I showed them how I'd escaped and we noticed the fist-marks in the front door which he must have punched when he realised I'd gone. They had literally indented the hard mahogany door and its frame.

In the shed the Detectives were stunned by the number of tools on the walls. There were two stolen cars and a jeep. And of course there was the motorbike, the green Kawasaki 750 that had been used for the murder. In the back room behind the wooden stud wall, I showed them the pool table and the bar where the parties had happened. Outside, reinforcements had been brought in to search the fields. It was raining that morning and I was soaked through but I had a lot to show them. I think many of them felt I was leading them on a merry dance and some of them commented loud enough for me to hear that I was just a "scrote". I showed them first where I had left the gun under a tuft of grass. They surrounded it and placed tape around it. One officer photographed it. I could hear all the phones going and there was a sense of excitement. "We've got the gun," they were telling their colleagues. The ones who had made the nasty comments about me were on their mobiles too. I wondered whether their opinion of me changed.

We walked back around the top field where I showed them where I'd buried the money, the smack and the coke. Each time they hauled up another black bag full of cash or drugs they marked it, photographed it and then filed it as evidence. We walked for hours while I pointed out the flasks and the containers hidden in the ditches, in the hedgerows and in the makeshift graves I had dug. I directed them to the gateposts where I had stored smack in the Rubik's cubes. By the time we were finished I had handed up around €200,000 of Brian Kenny's cash and probably the same amount again in smack and coke. I showed them the stolen boat and the jet skis and anything else I could think of that he had stashed away. Cold, wet, hungry and exhausted, Toddy and his men bundled me back into a car and made for Ballymun and Ma's house. I didn't even realise I was going home until I got there. I had no idea I was saying goodbye. As we pulled up people seemed to come out on the street from everywhere. Niamh met me at the door, tears streaming down her face. She embraced me and rocked me from side to side. She'd packed me a bag with some clothes and toiletries. Ma hugged me and pushed some money into my hand. "You'll need a few bob, Joseph. We love you."

As I walked back out to the cop car I remember Ma roaring at all the spectators and telling them to mind their own "fuckin'" business. I almost laughed as it was so strange to hear Ma curse. At the end of the road, standing around the van where the women bought their groceries, some of my friends stood and watched me pass. Familiar faces faded into the distance but I knew that soon they'd all know what I did, that I had broken an unwritten code, an *omertà*.

Back at the station Brian denied everything and laughed at the suggestion that I had told them anything at all. "We have Joey," officers repeatedly told him but he'd grin and shake his head. I was told later that he was demanding to see certain officers and throwing names about, but he was told in no uncertain terms that nobody could help him with the charges he was facing. Apparently the colour only drained from his face when the gun, still covered in dirt and grass, was placed on the table in front of him. Hinchon was missing and an army of Gardai were out looking for him.

Later in a hotel room under the protection of an armed guard, I met two more detectives who told me that I'd have to give much longer statements. A doctor was called to examine the bruises and marks that covered my body. In a full-length mirror I caught a glimpse of myself for the first time in months. I was gaunt and my eyes looked frightened and were sunk into the back of my head. I looked just like a junkie with my clothes hanging off me and my body like a bag of bones.

I tried to sleep but I couldn't. Every time I closed my eyes terror would engulf me and the enormity of what I had done would weigh down on me, leaving me short of breath and soaking with sweat. I felt guilt and remorse. I wondered how Brian was doing in his cell away from Mandy. I would forget for a minute where I was, my mind wandering off to some distant memory, but then my body would jerk like I'd fallen from a height and the sweating and shakes would start again.

CHAPTER 9

Eventually I was prescribed medication to help with the panic attacks and the anxiety but it didn't work.

Detectives came and went and I was given support and encouragement; but we came from very different worlds and try as they might to make me feel we were in it together, the time always came when they could go home to their families and I could not. A debate raged in my head. Had I done the right thing or the wrong thing? I'd never met them but I knew that Jonathan O'Reilly's family deserved the truth about how Jonathan had been taken from them. At the same time I was so scared and I couldn't help but regret leaving rather than facing my fate too. Every time I was alone I'd panic about what I'd done but then I'd speak to Ma and the fog and the doubts would clear. Her absolute moral code about right and wrong was so reassuring.

One morning I went downstairs in my safe house to find Toddy waiting for me with some news. Kenny had applied for bail and I needed to go to court and give evidence against him. I couldn't believe it. I was still so broken yet I somehow had to find the strength to face him down. "You'll be fine Joe. Just go in and tell the truth. We'll be with you. He won't be able to hurt you," Toddy told me. A few hours later I was waiting outside the Cloverhill Courthouse surrounded by Gardai, and ready to face Brian directly for the first time since I'd fled. I wasn't happy about giving evidence but my choices were pretty limited. If I went ahead I was to go on the Witness Protection

Programme. I would receive a new identity and help settling down to a new life after the trial. I would be granted immunity from prosecution myself for drug offences. I told them I'd do it, I'd sign up, but said I could never leave Ireland and if I was relocated afterwards, I'd still have to be able to see Ma.

I was terrified but determined that I had to do my best for the sake of Ma and Jonathan O'Reilly's family and all the other people who Brian had hurt and who I had let down by not speaking up. I had no idea the court would be so packed until I was sitting in the elevated witness box and looking out over a sea of at least 100 faces. In front of me I saw Billy and other members of his family staring me down. I looked right and there was Brian in a tracksuit bottom and sloppy top. He was jumping up and down staring at me like a madman. I turned my head to the judge and started to talk. I could see Brian out of the corner of my eye getting up and down and making a big scene until the judge eventually told him to stop and ordered the Gardai to stand in front of him so he couldn't see me. I told the judge about the day Jonathan was murdered and how Brian and Hinchon had threatened to kill me too. I told him I was scared and didn't know what I'd do if Brian Kenny was released on bail.

A detective who was in the court that day would later tell me that the minute I started to talk they all knew that I was going to convict the two killers. I had no idea what I was doing; I just told the truth. When I was finished the judge refused bail, telling Brian he was sure that if he was released, my life would be over. As I walked back out of the courtroom surrounded by the Gardai I could hear the whispers and the hisses. "Rat. Snitch... Rat."

Back in my safe house I remained under protection as the Witness Protection Programme process began. I had nothing. The Gardai couldn't give me anything because they couldn't be seen to be enticing me. They helped me sign on and collect my social welfare and in doing so discovered that Brian had been claiming rent allowance for me so I could live at Mitchelstown Cottage. There was a car in my name and my brother sold it for me so I made some money from that. I was pretty bored and having so much time on my hands made me even more anxious. Someone brought me a PlayStation and I found the mindless repetition of the games soothing.

When the bureaucratic process of the Witness Protection Programme had been completed I was suddenly passed to new handlers. I didn't like one of them from the minute I met him. They came to collect me in a car and on the way to my new safe house, the officer pulled in and parked up. I didn't know what was happening. He turned around. "You got a phone?" he asked. "Yes. I have it here," I said. "Well give it to me then." I handed him my phone, the only thing I had left to myself. He took the back off it, took out the SIM, stared at me and then snapped it in two. Tossing me a new phone he said, "You're on my rules now." I don't know why he had to behave like that.

This was my life and I didn't need some idiot pretending he was in a movie. The rest of the guys were nice and they kind of let me know they thought he was a twit too.

The new regime was stricter than before. I was put into an apartment where I was pretty much expected to stay all day. I couldn't talk to my handlers about the trial or about Brian. I couldn't contact anyone unless it was through my handlers. I was alone for the first time in my whole life and felt lonely and totally overwhelmed. Very early on I was taken to see a therapist who would become my lifeline. The first time we met we seemed to get on well. She was attractive with dark hair and was dressed like a lawyer in a sharp business suit and high heels. She told me I could talk to her about anything I wanted. For someone who had grown up in a house full of women I think I found it easier to relate to her than I did some of the burly cops who were around me all the time. So many of them were really kind and nice to me but I always found it easier to talk to a woman about my feelings; the therapist filled the void that signing on the Witness Protection Programme had created. It felt good to start to unravel all my confusing feelings about Brian. Our meetings became the most important thing in my life. Of course it wasn't until years later that I was told I should have been seeing a psychiatrist rather than just a therapist, but that was not offered to me.

As the weeks wore on I settled down a little bit. One very decent Garda encouraged me to do my Junior Certificate and he registered me for the exams and brought me all the books. He actually gave me private lessons in English, History, Maths and Geography and was so kind and patient with me. He didn't have to do that. He did it because he was a good person and he restored some of my trust in humanity. I passed all of my exams and got an A in English and three Cs. I met Ma at special locations and we went for walks and sometimes had a bit of lunch and a chat while we were kept under surveillance. She'd tell me all her news and I'd tell her mine. I saw Niamh and Louise once or twice too and spoke to them on the phone. I struggled a lot with my feelings about Brian. One minute I would be raging about him and the violence he subjected me too. Then I'd be overwhelmed by sadness and I'd remember him telling people I was like his son. I'd think about him in prison and how badly he'd be coping with that. Then I'd think of the beatings. And I would think about the rapes.

Christmas came and went and I got to see Ma. The Gardai had all sorts of tricks when it came to getting us together and making sure I could see my family as often as possible. I they definitely did their best and some of them went above and beyond the call of duty with their kindness to us. But it was never really enough. I was totally incapable of being on my own or being without Ma. I felt I had regressed since leaving Brian's and I needed her with me all the time. I had a cake for my 20th birthday in my sister's house and spent a few hours with my family, but weeks would go by without a visit. One of my handlers helped me see my daughter which was a huge thing. I just couldn't believe that anyone would do that for me. He also used to drop in for a cup of tea when he could.

Only those people who've actually been on the Witness Protection Programme can understand the loneliness, and how long the days and nights can feel when you are waiting and hiding. I moved safe houses a number of times. I knew nobody and had nothing to do. I felt depressed and totally isolated. I started to drink vodka and chew Solpadeine as well as taking more tablets than I was prescribed. My handlers joined me in a gym but the silence was suffocating me.

Seeing my therapist became the most important thing in my life. She told me I had to ask to see her or speak to her whenever I wanted but she couldn't ask to see me. It never even crossed my mind she was being paid; I always seemed a special case for her. She was British so she couldn't always come to Ireland to see me but if I asked for her they'd get her on the phone; I very quickly became hugely reliant on her. I told her everything about Brian and started to see the extent of his control over me and how he had used psychological, physical and sexual abuse to make me do his bidding. She was oddly open about herself and her marriage difficulties. She told me she had started a relationship with one of my handlers, the one I didn't like, and was always asking me about him. She told me that he didn't like his boss, who was another one of my handlers, and was after information from me; I

CHAPTER 9

didn't really have the mental capacity to listen to it all. I had enough problems of my own without my therapist offloading onto me.

One night I was asleep in one of the apartments when my phone started to ring like crazy. I was groggy from vodka and pills but when I answered, the handler told me that Hinchon had put together a hit squad to kill me. The Gardai were trying to find them and arrest them but I needed to move quickly. I was removed from the apartment within minutes and the arrests were made. I believe the members of the squad admitted they were under instructions to kill me.

I was then moved again, this time far into the midlands to a town I had never visited before. The pressure of this precarious life really started getting to me. The trial was looming but the only person I could talk to about it was my therapist. At night I drank myself to oblivion. By day I pulled the duvet over my head. The world seemed to be closing in around me. I knew that the trial was approaching fast and that everyone was relying on me. My evidence would be vital if Brian and Hinchon were to be convicted of murder and I just hoped I could hold it together until the time came. One afternoon I was in a car with one of the handlers when a news item on the radio reported that Brian Kenny and Thomas Hinchon had pleaded not guilty to the gangland murder of Jonathan O' Reilly. I was shocked. Nobody had told me the trial had started; I suppose they weren't allowed to. The trial, the news report said, was expected to last two weeks and would hear evidence from the state witness Joseph O'Callaghan. This was it. It was game on: the biggest day of my life lay ahead.

Joey, wearing a bullet proof vest, looks to speak to politicians outside Dail Eireann after his return to Ireland and his beating on Dublin's Quays.

CHAPTER 10

"Are you Joseph O'Callaghan?" The registrar's words seemed to echo around the courtroom despite the fact it was packed to capacity. It was standing room only and a sea of faces looked up at me from the body of the court below. "I am, your honour," I said, addressing the judge, Justice Michael Peart. I shifted around in the wooden chair and leaned in to the skinny little microphone in front of me. Even though I was refusing to look at them I could feel the stares of Brian Kenny and Thomas Hinchon drilling into me from the dock to my left. They were so close that if I reached out my arm I could have touched them. Across the courtroom were the jury – 10 men and two women of varying shapes and ages, staring at me intently. One of the women was around the same age as Ma and she looked kind. I knew they would have been told who I was during the opening speeches and no doubt my role in the finding of the gun had been well and truly detailed. Apart from that they would have known nothing about me and these were the people who would

CHAPTER 10

decide not only the fate of Kenny and Hinchon but also mine. In telling the Garda all I knew about the murder I had played a risky game of roulette and put everything I had on black. If the ball ended up on red I was a dead man; nothing could save me. I had no secrets up my sleeve, no smoking gun. All that was between me and a bullet in the head was the truth. I really hoped that was enough.

The court clerk handed me a Bible and told me to stand. I took it and repeated after her "I swear to almighty God that the evidence I shall give shall be the truth, the whole truth and nothing but the truth. So help me God." I meant every word of that sacred pledge. I had done bad things during my time with Brian, but this was my confession and while he was in the dock pleading not guilty to murder, I knew that I was on trial too. For the first time in my life I felt I had a chance against him. He wasn't going to be able to play his usual games in a courtroom and the jury looked pretty switched on to me. Since I'd heard on the radio that the trial was underway, my every waking moment had been consumed with thoughts of the evidence I was going to give. The night in Ballymun Garda station seemed a lifetime away but I was crystal-clear about what had happened the day that Jonathan O'Reilly was murdered. Despite it being a little over a year since I had led the Gardai around Mitchelstown Cottage and its surrounding fields, I could remember every ditch I showed them and every step we took.

From watching television shows and reading the papers I guessed that once I had told the court what had happened, my past would be thrown up at me. I had no idea how bad the next few days were going to be and there were no words that could have prepared me. From my perch I quickly scanned the crowd. I saw that Billy, Peter Joyce and Mandy were at the back. Some of Hinchon's young lads who had been over at Mitchelstown Cottage were scattered around. Each one of them glared at me with looks of pure hatred; there was no doubting I was the enemy now. Below me sat a row of men and women in suits with their backs to me and across a wide table from them were a row of lawyers, dressed in black capes and wigs. Neatly bound books marked "photographs" lay on the table, along with files and folders full of typed pages. Behind them were another row of lawyers also dressed in wigs, with mounds of papers on the desks in front of them. In another part of the courtroom I spotted the journalists, pens and notebooks in hand and bottles of water on the benches beside them. It was clearly going to be a long day. Towards the back of the court sat a row of people with a framed picture on the bench beside them. I jolted a little. They were obviously Jonathan O'Reilly's family and whatever I was feeling, they must have been feeling it 10 million times worse.

Despite the time it had taken the case to get to court I was still the youngest ever person to sign up to the Witness Protection Programme. I had turned 20 but I still looked a lot younger than my years. In the suit that Ma had bought me for the court case I looked as respectable as I ever had in my life, but I wasn't sure if I was going to manage to keep the tie on as it already felt like it was choking me. I took a deep breath and turned my attention to the judge who looked down at the lawyer with the wig nearest to me. I had only ever given evidence once before against Brian's application for bail, and that had happened in a bit of a blur. I knew, however, that the bloke standing up was the senior counsel for the prosecution and he would be taking me through the evidence I was giving to the court. I also knew this would be the easy bit. Across the table, the two sets of defence counsels representing Hinchon and Kenny took out their pens and started to chat amongst themselves. I wondered to myself who was paying for all these lawyers.

You could hear a pin drop in the courtroom as the prosecution counsel, a balding man with tiny glasses, introduced himself as Mr Shane Murphy and started to ask me about my early life, where I had lived and how I had met Brian Kenny. By and large I was able to answer "Yes" to most of his questions. He recounted the details about my job on the milk float and how I came to start living at Mitchelstown Cottage. I corrected him a few times and added a few details as I started to relax a little bit into the chair. I admitted that I had sold drugs but made sure to point out that I did it all for Brian Kenny. The details of my teenage years were grim and I was very self-conscious about it all, but there was no way

I was going to tell one single lie under oath. I knew this was the only chance I would get to tell the truth.

While I knew that my Garda handlers were in the courtroom and that Ma was waiting for me, I had never felt more alone than when I was in that box. I was very determined, however, and when we got to the day of Jonathan O'Reilly's murder, I could see Hinchon and Brian out of the corner of my eye. Hinchon was throwing his head back and forward as if he was 'goofing off', while Kenny was sat bolt upright and undoubtedly hanging on my every word. He had a notebook and pen and it looked like he was frantically writing things down.

I described how the pair of them had gone out on the morning of April 17 the previous year and then returned to the shed, where they had told me that they had shot "a fella" outside Cloverhill prison. I said I had checked the Aertel news stream which initially said the victim was seriously injured before later revealing that he had died. "When it said he wasn't dead, they were worried," I told the court. I said Kenny had asked me to hide the gun and described how I ran to the far corner of the field. I described how I had hidden it and covered it with leaves and marked the spot with a few sticks which I had made into a cross. I looked at the jury and told them that I was scared of Brian. "I felt afraid... Brian Kenny told me he shot yer man, that he'd done it once and he'd no problem doing it again... He said he'd kill me if I opened my mouth... I didn't know what to do, I was afraid."

CHAPTER 10

I told them that a few days after the murder Kenny had asked me to drive him to a house in Clondalkin where he spoke to a woman before coming out the side passage with the green motorbike they had left Mitchelstown Cottage on that day. I told them about going up to the airport to torch the other items with petrol and a lit sock. "How did you feel about the whole incident?" the lawyer asked me. I looked over at the jury. "I wanted to go home to my Ma," I said. I didn't care who was listening and I ignored the sniggers in the courtroom and beside me from the dock. I really didn't care what Brian and Hinchon and their cohorts thought about me.

I told the court about my escape, how Louise came for me in the car and going with Ma to Ballymun Garda station. I gave evidence until the end of the afternoon session, at which point the judge decided to send the jury and me home to start again in the morning. I was walked back out of the courtroom and into the back area reserved for the judiciary, where the Gardai met me and took me back to the safe house. I stayed on my own that night. As I was still sworn in I couldn't speak to anybody about my evidence. It was a long and lonely night. The following morning I was driven back to the courtroom and returned to the witness box. The courtroom was no less crowded but I avoided eye contact as much as I could with all the people straining their necks to get a good look at me. Painstakingly we went through how I led the Gardai to the gun and the drugs and cash buried in the fields around Mitchelstown Cottage and then to what was left of the helmets and the leathers. When the state prosecutor announced his questions were over and handed me over to the defense, I believed I would be there for another few hours. I had no idea that I was going to be grilled to within an inch of my life. Brian shifted in his seat beside me as if he was about to stand up. But he was only sitting forward to watch the show. This was his moment.

The defense went straight for the jugular. "Mr O'Callaghan, you have complete immunity from prosecution for possession of drugs. Is that correct?" Brian's lawyer was John Phelan, an elderly man with grey hair, a beard and piercing blue eyes. He was really posh and came across as very clever. He had smiled at the jury as he told them how I had been arrested for possession of heroin worth €160 in 2003. "That's true yeah," I answered him. He seemed a bit surprised. The arrest had been a small matter compared to everything else I had got up to under Brian's direction, particularly during that last crazy year at Mitchelstown Cottage. "You are free as a bird from these drug charges, Mr O'Callaghan, isn't that right? You were facing serious charges, now suddenly you are giving evidence pointing the guilt at my client. There are three documents supporting you that no prosecution will take place. You are as safe as a house, you will not be prosecuted now or in the future." Mr Phelan swept around dramatically to look at the jury.

"Yeah, that's right," I said. "But that doesn't mean I'm not telling the truth about Jonathan O'Reilly's murder." The old man sort of grinned but I held his eye. Weirdly Brian had told his lawyer a lot of the details of his heroin business and the robberies, but he had left out one vital detail: that he was personally involved. Instead the lawyer recounted a fairy tale of how Brian had plucked me from the streets of Blanchardstown after I had got into trouble hanging out with Shane Coates and Stephen Sugg and was on my way to becoming a key member of the Westies. He put it to me that Brian had offered me kindness and given me work and taken me under his wing but I had been unable to put my criminal ways behind me. He claimed that behind his back I had started to knock around with the Bradleys and with Martin Marlo Hyland. He even suggested that Operation Anvil, a huge Garda offensive against Hyland, was actually targeted at me and my "drug-dealing gang". I almost laughed but I apologised to the judge and jury and told Mr Phelan he couldn't have been more wrong.

He said that "Mr Kenny" had tried very hard to keep me on the straight and narrow but I had been drug-dealing and robbing at will. "Yeah, I did those things. I did them. But he made me do them," I said, pointing at Brian. When he suggested that I had killed Jonathan O'Reilly and then blamed him and Hinchon to save my own skin, I told him his claims were ridiculous. "Why then did I bring the Gardai to the gun and the bike? Why are there text messages on my phone when I was in the Garda station from him looking for his gun back?

Why was he threatening to kill me and my family? Because he done it, that's why. He murdered Jonathan O'Reilly." "I'll ask the questions, Mr O'Callaghan," the lawyer said, but I found it hard to excuse him for that accusation.

Still he continued, at one point putting it to me that I had tried to frame Brian Kenny and his pal for murder because I fancied Mandy. I felt like saying that there were easier ways to get a shag but stopped myself out of respect for the court. Besides, the argument made no sense really and I think the more ludicrous the scenarios that were presented, the less the jury were inclined to take the defense seriously. I batted back each allegation and tried to argue using common sense and truth. "Why would I do that? That doesn't make sense," I kept repeating, but the lawyer would just get annoyed. I could tell from his entire line of questioning that Phelan was acting completely on Brian Kenny's instructions. I could hear the influence of his twisted mind coming through in the allegations against me and in the way he tried to blame everything he had done on me. I hoped that the jury would also realise this, but they didn't know Brian like I did. The cross-examination took days. Each morning and afternoon I sat down in the witness box and prepared for mental battle. Each day the court was packed and I felt like I was on display for the whole of Dublin to see. I was exhausted by the time Brian's lawyer was concluding but I hadn't let him get away with a single thing. "You present yourself as the picture of innocence, Mr O'Callaghan. I have to suggest to you that you are a criminal." Phelan again swept around to look at the jury and from somewhere deep inside me came a reply: "Not anymore, I'm changed. I've changed for good." I'd never meant any words more in my life.

Phelan must have been worn out himself by the time he sat down but he was really only handing over the baton. Hinchon's lawyer was next. He looked like something from an old Agatha Christie book. Towering at six foot, his wiry grey hair stuck out under his yellowed wig and he sported a matching moustache. Small half spectacles stood on the tip of his nose and his fingers felt around the pocket of his waistcoat where a pipe stuck out. In a powerful voice he started to ask me about the teletext reports and the time of day when I had read about the shooting. I insisted it was around 5.30pm but he said that Garda inquiries suggested it would have been nearer 7pm when the news was run on TV3's service. He then went into detail about the times the news had come up on RTE and tried to tie me into knots. "You are telling me lies," he said, but I could see that the jury weren't exactly seeing it as a smoking gun. He went back over my drug offence and my immunity and claimed that I had only implicated Hinchon because he was a friend of Brian's. Eventually he finished up and the judge told me I could step down from the witness box. It was a Friday and I thought I was finished, but on the following Monday, Phelan requested that I be brought back again for more. I couldn't believe it but I had never thought it was going to be easy.

Back in the witness box he asked me again about supplying heroin and how I had told the Gardai about it. I admitted it was true but he then went on to bring up how my car had been seized because it hadn't been taxed or insured and how I had run away from the Gardai. This did happen in the weeks after the murder but I barely registered it at the time. "This was a strange thing to do, Mr O'Callaghan," the barrister said, squinting his eyes at me. I squinted back. "Not where I come from. You see the guards and you run," I said. He went on to claim I had told Mandy I was worried about the car before asking me whether I had been touting to a drug squad officer leading to raids on friends' houses. Again Brian was projecting onto me but in doing so was making the ridiculous suggestion that I had framed him for murder because I was worried about my car.

"You are a self-confessed criminal, Mr O'Callaghan, and you wouldn't know the truth if it jumped up and bit you. You made this nonsense up, you concocted it up to save your own skin." I waited until he was finished and looked him straight in the eye. He was only doing his job but he sounded so stupid to me. "You don't accuse people of murder because your car is being taken, this is 2005, get real... Just because I don't have tax and insurance, that I would accuse someone of murder – get a life."

I hoped I'd done enough. I couldn't even consider the possibility that I hadn't. The jury were sent out and I got a hefty Garda escort away from the courts for the last time. Back in my safe house I played on my computer and watched television. I waited and I waited and I waited for what seemed like an eternity. All sorts of scenarios went through my head. What was I actually going to do if they got off? How far away was going to be far enough away from the wrath of Brian Kenny? Did a place like that even exist? That evening, word came from the courts that the jury had found Brian guilty of possession of a firearm and ammunition. These were the lesser charges but it suggested they believed me. They had gone to a hotel for the night and would continue their deliberations on the murder charges the following day. Tuesday dragged on but that evening just as I thought it was going to drag into another day I received a phone call. The jury had found Brian guilty of murder and both him and Hinchon guilty of threatening to kill me. They had been sent to a hotel again and were expected to conclude their deliberations the following morning on the remaining count of murder against Hinchon. But I knew he was gone too. They had believed me about Brian and there was no reason they wouldn't believe me about Hinchon. In total it took them 15 hours to convict him too. The relief was unbelievable. I was in no mood to celebrate, I just collapsed. I turned on the news and it was the top story.

The next day Hinchon was also found guilty of murder and news sites were running the full court reports. I stared at the headline: "Two get life for Cloverhill murder." The report described the details of the shooting, the evidence that Robbie O'Hanlon had given about needing to drop something off at Cloverhill that day, and the circumstances around the arrests. It also recounted a lot of my evidence, reporting that the judge had told Hinchon and Kenny that it was "as cold, calculated and premeditated a slaying of a young man as can be imagined." The judge had expressed his sympathy with Jonathan's family who he said would continue to suffer for a long time. I wondered how they were feeling. They had nothing to celebrate either: Jonathan was still gone. Outside the court Toddy gave an interview to journalists who referred to him by his full title: Detective Inspector Thomas O'Loughlin. He said the guilty verdicts sent out a clear message to people involved in crime that they weren't immune to prosecution and investigation and they would ultimately end up before the courts. "Mr O'Callaghan was extremely afraid for his life. As a result he is currently in the Witness Protection Programme and will remain so," he remarked. I've no doubt that he believed what he was saying but others had different ideas about my future. Within months of my celebrated evidence I would be alone, cast adrift and on a downhill spiral to a hell I had never previously known. I was about to find out what it is like to outlive your usefulness.

Some say that the best way to remove a sticking plaster is with one quick, sharp tug. Whether that is true is debateable, but it was certainly the way the Gardai in charge of my case dealt with me when my protection came to an end. I had been on an emotional rollercoaster ever since stepping down from the witness box that final time. Jonathan O'Reilly's family, so relieved about the verdicts, had not been permitted to meet me so wrote me a letter instead, enclosed with a picture of Jonathan in a gold frame with the words "always with you xxxx" written underneath. There was also a little picture for my wallet and a personalised keyring showing his face and with his name written on the back. The letter was just lovely. They thanked me for my bravery and for doing the right thing and assured me that my giving evidence had lifted the burden of his death. They described how full of life Jonathan was and how devastated they all were that he had been taken away in his prime with his whole life ahead of him. They described the amazing relationship he had with his son and how the child would now have to grow up without a father because of the evil deed that Brian Kenny and Thomas Hinchon carried out that April day. They wished me happiness in my life and assured me that they appreciated everything I had done. It was a beautiful letter and I cried as I read it but I wasn't allowed to keep it in case anyone ever found it. I just about convinced my handlers to let me keep the picture and the little keyring. I promised that I would claim he was an old friend or relative who had died if anyone should ask.

Very quickly negotiations about my exit from the programme began. I was in turmoil. Some of the handlers disagreed about what was best for me and my future. I think one side realised how vulnerable I was and believed I needed to be built up mentally before I could be cut loose. Unfortunately the opposing camp prevailed. There were rows and disagreements and I didn't know which way to turn. In the middle of it I tried to take my life. Overwhelmed by the idea of being away from my family, a blackness came over me and one night I took a load of tablets. I woke up in a hospital bed where my stomach had been pumped and where I was told I was lucky to be alive. I didn't feel very lucky.

Once recovered I was taken to a solicitor's office to sign out of the programme. The therapist accompanied me and reassured me that I was doing the right thing. She told me her boyfriend, the handler I didn't like, was moving to the UK and they were going to set up a business together once he retired. She said if I moved to the UK I would have better access to her once I got settled. I got the impression that if I was in the UK she would be better placed to look after my needs and that I would be part of their circle of friends. I had no concept of how weird or inappropriate that was at the time. But for me it was a lifeline, someone familiar, a person that I knew.

There was constant talk about money but nobody seemed to understand that I had never done any of it for that. In contrast to Brian, I had never made anything out of my years with him and really I had no concept or interest in money. Although I was now 20 years old, I had never paid a bill or had a bank account and didn't even know the price of groceries.

CHAPTER 10

I realise now that nobody who dealt with my exit agreement from the Programme had any idea how badly equipped I was mentally to be on my own.

The deal was eventually done although I felt I had no control over it whatsoever. In my case I literally had to sign away my life agreeing to a new identity, a new background history and a new start in a new country and city where I knew nobody. I wasn't allowed any contact or communication with anyone I had previously known. I couldn't even contact Ma. And that was to be forever. Saying goodbye to her in the car park of a hotel in Dublin was the hardest thing I had ever done. The police gave us 10 minutes as they waited nearby to take me to the airport. It was surreal and I boarded my flight in a daze, my whole life in the small cabin bag I wheeled behind me.

In my new base I longed for home. In the strangeness of the environment I masked my emotions and tried hard to settle down and fit in. I first rented an apartment before buying a cheap property. I signed up to college where I studied to be a care worker. I got a job in a centre for people with mental health difficulties as I completed course after course. I liked the work but I was lonely and isolated. My only contact with my past was with my therapist who I regularly visited in London where I would meet up with her and my old handler. Their relationship was clearly flourishing. I spoke to her on the phone and emailed her but all the time I was running up a pretty hefty bill. Whenever I'd meet them, my ex-handler would take me to the bank and I'd withdraw thousands in cash and give it to him. While I had more money than I had ever had in my life, I simply hadn't a clue how to handle it. I'd often give it away to people I met and felt sorry for. I'd buy rounds of drinks for gangs of people I didn't even know in pubs, which I thought was normal. I'd purchase ridiculously extravagant pieces of jewellery or clothes which I didn't need or want. I'd sometimes buy the same things over and over again. Food would go off and go into the bin, credit card bills would sit unpaid despite the fact that I had enough to clear them. Ma would later tell me that she had begged the Gardai to let her manage my finances but they had refused.

I kept the photograph of Jonathan close to my heart and often at night as I drowned my loneliness in a bottle of vodka, I would talk to him and ask him to look after me. Danger and the realities of the underworld were never far away. Weeks after Kenny and Hinchon had been sentenced to life imprisonment, names from my past were all over the news. Andrew Chiccore Dillon, who had been there that first time I met Marlo Hyland, was shot dead and dumped in a ditch in north Dublin. His assassination was terrifying and very cold-blooded. Chiccore had been one of Marlo's heavies but he had obviously gone a step too far with someone. His murder only merited a short article online, and nobody had even bothered to use a picture of him. Life had become very cheap indeed in the underworld that I had once inhabited. Weeks later Mark Glennon was top of the news. His brother Andrew had only been dead a few months when he was shot dead in the garden of his home. Everyone knew the Glennons from their association and later fall out with the Westies. They had gone to my school but were older than me so I only knew them by reputation. But I was interested to read that like me, they had moved to Blanchardstown from Ballymun when they were young boys. I wondered how they had got involved in the drug scene, whether they had been lured in or whether they had chosen their path in life. I thought of their parents and what it must have been like to lose two children in such violent circumstances.

My own fear of being shot dead was all-encompassing. If I could get to sleep at all, I'd wake at night in a pool of sweat convinced someone was coming for me. My dreams were filled with images of Hinchon and Kenny wandering about my college campus looking for me. I had constant flashbacks of being beaten and whipped. My terror of being tracked down grew and grew to unrealistic proportions. Sometimes I would see people looking at me and become convinced they had been sent from Ireland. I'd sprint off all the time, jumping walls and rounding corners like I was being hunted. I turned my home into a fortress, paying a fortune to install a top-of-the-range CCTV system and reinforced windows. I kept two cars and changed them constantly, losing thousands in the process. I kept to myself and was afraid of everyone. I'd been given a name and the number of a local cop to ring should I need anything, but when I tried, I was told he had retired and could do nothing for me. Despite receiving extensive therapy while I was on the Programme and clearly needing it going forward, nothing had been set up for me. My own arrangements with the therapist were all I had. I wasn't in a position to rock up at some counselling service and tell people that I had been a protected witness. That would blow everything, yet I wasn't given anything else.

Away from home too I was tormented with thoughts of the trial and everything that had happened with Brian. I knew I could never go back to the life that I had known and that my community, and even some of my own flesh and blood, would never be able to see past the fact that I was now a rat. To this day I think many people simply don't understand the seriousness of ratting. Within many working class communities there is actually no more serious offence you can commit. You can murder or maim, take money from sick junkies while they pump their veins with your drugs and even beat a man to a pulp, but woe betide you if you give any information to the Gardai. The *omertà* is an unwritten code. And while it is illogical beyond reason, it is also sacred and there is no going back from breaking it. But my choices were limited. What exactly was I supposed to do? Should Brian

Kenny have been allowed get away with murder? Should I have kept my mouth shut? Then I'd look at the picture of Jonathan and I would think of the words of his family and I would know I'd done the right thing.

The conflict inside my head was relentless. I raged at what had happened in my life, casting blame on everyone, even my Ma. I'd work it all out in my head that it had been her fault for making me go to the Gardai, that she was to blame for me now floating all alone on a never ending sea of misery. Then I'd come back from the darkness and I would feel so guilty for even thinking such things. I'd think of the rapes and the beatings and I'd get angry and sad and I'd cry and I'd scream and I'd punch the walls. Tormented by the lack of sleep, my sense of paranoia grew all the time and I started to display irrational behaviours. It would take me years to realise why this was happening. Some days I wouldn't leave the house and spend hours pacing the rooms looking out the windows. Other times I would go out and get drunk or coked up with strangers and find myself in all sorts of dangerous situations.

I had a huge tolerance to drugs as I had been taking them since I was 12 years old and I fell quickly back into a total reliance on them to get through each day. From the moment that Brian had given me my first Valium to help me come down from the cocaine, benzos had been my drug. I couldn't get enough of diazepam, alprazolam, lorazepam, you name it. I went to a number of different doctors with different stories and got multiple prescriptions so I could self-medicate. That feeling of my whole body and mind relaxing into a murky puddle was the only relief I got from the racing thoughts and anxiety attacks. I had been given a back story but it was fairly sparse. It had been formulated by the handler I didn't like. He had laughed when he told me my new name because it was the same as a famous gangster. I was supposed to be from a wealthy family in Dublin which would explain why a student had his own home and cars but looking back now I must have seemed such an oddity. It was a stupid story and it didn't make any sense.

Every time I would try to focus positively on the future, something seemed to happen to bring back my past and the road that had led to where I now was. In July 2006, less than a year after I had left Ireland, the bodies of my old neighbours, the Westies, were discovered in a concrete grave in Spain. Shane Coates and Stephen Sugg had been missing since just before Jonathan's murder. I had followed snippets about them that had appeared in the media but there had been no sign of them until someone had tipped off the gardai about their remains and they had informed their Spanish counterparts. I wondered who had given the information up and why? Like me had they been haunted by the loss of the Coates and Sugg families? Had they seen something unthinkable? Were they out there now like me, terrified, alone and climbing the walls? The stories on the internet said the Westies had gone to Spain for a slice of the action on the Costa Blanca, believing they could muscle in with their notorious reputations. But it appeared far more brutal characters than them had somehow lured them to their death and buried them, possibly alive. Their rise to gangland fame was recalled in graphic details. I thought about Adam and I wondered how he would feel reading it all. Shane was still his brother no matter what, and he had once been his hero.

Despite the rules I had kept in touch with Ma. I'd ring her from a phone box every few weeks and we had a code to indicate if she was unable to talk. She was the only one I'd ever speak to back home in all the years I was in England. I didn't tell her where I was living or how badly I was coping but I think she knew. Winter approached and with it my second Christmas alone with no family or friends to share a meal with. But just weeks beforehand the realities of the world I once lived in came hammering home yet again, this time with the murder of Marlo Hyland back in Dublin. The Godfather who had always seemed so untouchable to me was gone, shot dead as he slept in his bed. It was easy to see what had happened. Operation Oak, the Garda crackdown on his mob, had clearly been hugely successful and there was no doubt the 40 arrests, the hauls of heroin, cocaine and cannabis and the charges brought against more than 20 of his gang had caused his once powerful organisation to implode. I knew exactly how it worked and how paranoia could eat away at any gang. God knows, Marlo had probably been killed by one of his own.

An innocent plumber called Anthony Campbell who was only 18 had been murdered too because he was working there fixing a radiator. The lad looked so young and innocent in the pictures. He was just so unlucky to have been there at the time. I couldn't get him out of my head and I felt guilty for being alive. I consumed everything I could about Marlo's murder, every article I could find detailing how he died. I relived that first meeting with him when he got me to lay my hands on the table in front of him. I remembered his eyes, blue and cold, and how Brian had adored him. Marlo had been living between safe houses for the last year of his life but he had enemies who were determined to take him out. If a guy like Marlo couldn't survive, what hope had I?

During my second year in college I made a friend. He was a local guy and big into the drug scene. He was the last fella I should have gone near but I was somehow drawn to him. I went out with him one night and met his sister. She had just had a baby but had split from the father. We got on okay and I started seeing her but there was no really big spark there, no love at first sight, no songbirds. In fact if I'm honest the biggest connection we probably had was that we were both addicted to cocaine and tablets. I was way too numb and mentally unwell for any relationship but that didn't stop the destructive path I was on in life. She had her issues too but we kind of gravitated to each other, like two lost souls preferring to spend our nights taking drugs together than on our own. We'd party for nights on end on cocaine while her brother and his mates would smoke heroin. They often offered me smack but no matter how out of it I was, I'd never touch it. The smell of it reminded me of Brian and the gaunt look of the lads smoking it brought me back to the landings of Ballymun Towers.

Despite the mess my life was in, I let my girlfriend move in with me and very quickly she became pregnant. We both tried to clean ourselves up as we awaited the birth of our child. I hadn't been around to see my daughter being born or even for any of the pregnancy so I got really involved in the whole thing, tried hard to stay clean and started to consider a future as a proper family. But life was a lie. When my girlfriend would ask about the framed photograph on the mantelpiece, I'd tell her that Jonathan was my best friend who'd died from drugs. If she quizzed me about my family I told her I'd fallen out with them. I told her some of the truth as well, like the fact that my Da was dead, but I must have seemed so distant and strange. My frustrations would build up and I'd get really angry only to end up in floods of tears and not be able to tell anyone why I was upset. When I was alone I'd talk to Jonathan. I'd ask him to help me and look over me, just like his family had told me he would in their letter.

A few months before our child was born I suffered a series of setbacks which left me struggling to stay on the straight and narrow. While I had been attempting to settle in to my new life, I had been travelling up and down to London to see my therapist; sometimes she would visit me with my former handler. They were my only connection to my past and in my head she had become the most important human being in my life. I would have done anything for her and I thought we had a sort of "mother son" relationship. Her promise I'd be able to live beside her had kept me going through my darkest days, but as time wore on it had become clear there was no way that was going to happen. I felt let down all over again and pretty stupid. Eventually my phone calls and emails went unanswered and I knew I would never hear from either one of them again.

Back in Ireland the dark spectre of Jonathan's murder continued to loom over Clondalkin. In March 2007 Robbie O'Hanlon was shot dead. He was playing five-a-side football at the time, which must have been gruesome for anyone who witnessed it. Robbie had clearly set Jonathan up. He was supposed to be his friend but the Gardai knew early on that he had driven him to his death at Cloverhill Prison. I tried to remember his face but I couldn't. I only knew that Hinchon and Brian had talked about him a lot. I wondered how they would be feeling in jail on hearing the news. To them life was dispensable and cheap but I fretted that they would see it as even more reason to come after me.

My son was born that summer and I called him Jonathan. He was absolutely beautiful and for a little while I lived in a false dawn that ours was a happy family. But the demons returned and I reverted to the drugs and the oblivion they gave me. I was absent mentally. I'd stay awake for nights on end fuelled by cocaine, then come down on Benzos and sleep like I was hibernating. My relationship had no foundations, my life was a lie and I was soon to realise that if I didn't fix what was wrong inside me, I would never find peace. While I had spoken to Ma, I hadn't spoken to my sisters; I knew this upset them but I didn't want to put their lives under any more danger than I already had. I was consumed by guilt about everyone in my past and my present. Ma was bitter and angry with how I had been signed off the Programme. She said she had warned them that I wouldn't survive on my own and I think she sensed I was sliding further and further into the abyss. A year after Robbie O'Hanlon was shot dead, Richie McCormack was shot dead on the street by a lone gunman. He was another of Hinchon's crew and his car had been found in front of Mitchelstown Cottage on the morning of the raids. It seemed everyone I had once known was dying. Everyone except me. Each time there was a shooting I'd worry for Ma, for Niamh, for Louise and Natalie and for anyone else close to me back home.

As the dark clouds continued to gather, I began to lose everything: my job, my relationship and my sanity. Locked in my room all day, I self-medicated on tablets. I locked the doors over and over again, circling the house and checking them hundreds of times. I used what little money I had left to bulk buy household items. Toilet rolls, bottles of washing up liquid and jars of coffee were all stacked up like I was expecting a nuclear winter. I just didn't seem to be able to stop. My girlfriend knew nothing about what was going on in my head; she just thought I was mad. When she had an affair I blamed her for the relationship breakdown, but in hindsight neither of us were fit to be parents or to provide a stable home together.

Back home Eamon The Don Dunne had become the new psycho. I could hardly believe how he had risen through the ranks to become the most feared figure in gangland. I remembered him flogging gear for Marlo and bringing coke to the parties. He loved the sniff himself but it was extraordinary how dangerous he had become. Reading between the lines I could tell that he had been the one to order Marlo's death, before going on to wipe out many of those loyal to him. Lads like John Daly and Paul Farmer Martin were next to die, both in a hail of bullets. I had partied with them many a time in the Bradleys' shed. They were killed by lone gunmen who made quick getaways. Nobody had seen them come and nobody had seen them go.

After the breakup I was lonelier than ever in England but I now had something else to face up to. As I approached my 25th birthday I realised that there were many reasons that my first proper relationship hadn't worked out and it wasn't just the chaos of our lives. So much of my developing years had been stolen by Brian Kenny that I was only really beginning to realise that I was in fact a gay man. For so long my whole sexuality had been tied up with Brian Kenny's treatment of me, with the sexual abuse he had subjected me to and with the awful threats he made to me. I was only 14, a child, The first time Brian had sexually assaulted me I was only 14, a child, but I had almost become normalised to it. As the abuse turned to rape he had used the shed as cover, first from Rita and later from Mandy. I hated each and every time. The pain was inexplicable. He had constantly made out as if he was doing me a favour, setting me up for later life. He had called me "gay", "a faggot" or a "homo". Yet at the same time he had engaged me in crude conversations about girls that he thought I wanted to be with. At one point when a prostitute owed him money, he told her to pay me in kind and sent me off in a car with her. I was never going to do anything with the poor girl; she was in bits and had children at home. She was out selling her body to pay him for her drugs. She had asked me what I wanted her to do and I told her she didn't have to do anything, just pretend. Of course you can never trust a drug addict and she only went back and told Brian, and he ridiculed me over it. Brian himself was always enjoying the services of the hookers when they were at the drug parties. And yet he had to rape me too, I just couldn't understand it. With time and space to think about it all I found myself in mental turmoil. I hated myself for allowing it to happen and for going back to Brian every time. I blamed myself for not fighting harder against it. I wondered whether I deserved it and wanted it, but at the same time it made me so angry that he had done it. It would take me a long time to realise that it was all about power, control and humiliation and had nothing to do with sex. I knew I could never be free of Brian and if this life I was living was freedom then I didn't want it. I slipped further and further into despair, hopelessness and distress. I seemed to be just living to die.

The black dog came one night and before I knew it I was waking up in hospital having taken a massive overdose. I was in a bad way, probably the worst I had ever been. Coming too, I started to talk to nurses and doctors and care workers. I told anyone who would listen about my false name and my real name, about my false life and my real life. I told them about the hitmen who were out looking for me and how they were drawing closer all the time. I told them about Mitchelstown Cottage and the fields full of money and cocaine. My story must have sounded like the ramblings of a madman because I was sectioned to a psychiatric hospital where I told them all about my therapist and asked them to ring her. It was then I realised she had been working under an assumed identity. In the real world outside the Witness Protection Programme, she didn't exist. Eventually they rang Ma and she very quietly made her way over. I broke down when I saw her. She held my hand and very gently she whispered into my ear, "Joseph, it's time to come home now."

Joey and his mother Mary taken in 2005 before he gave evidence at the murder trials of Brian Kenny and Thomas Hinchon.

CHAPTER 11

I came home in the winter, flying into Belfast and making my way to Ma's house lying across the back seat of a car, a blanket covering my head. For weeks I stayed inside her flat, slowly detoxing my body. I vomited. I soiled myself. I cried. Eventually I was well enough to go to the Gardai to tell them I was back. It was the same station and the same middle-of-the-night call but this time they weren't interested in what I had to say. They told me no protection was available and I wasn't safe back home. Essentially they were done with me, unless I turned up in a ditch somewhere with a bullet in the head, a fairly likely occurrence.

I turned 25 two weeks after John Paul Joyce's frozen body was found in a ditch near Dublin Airport not far from Mitchelstown Cottage. I remembered Joyce well. He was one of the travellers that Brian had bought guns and cars from. He was violent, they said, and had made a lot of enemies, but he knew he was under threat and always wore a bullet proof vest. They got him anyway. I knew I couldn't stay at Ma's as it wasn't safe for her or fair on her, so I soon found a little bedsit in Cabra, less than 10 kilometres away. I had nothing and was forced to use my old identity records to claim social welfare so I could get by. A relative of my Da's who I trusted heard about my plight and offered me a job in their business. This suited me down to the ground. The job involved answering phones, writing up orders and staying in the background. It was perfect for keeping a low profile. I knew that to stay alive I would have to keep my wits about me; this meant staying off drugs so I signed up for rehabilitation and addiction services.

I was doing okay, but the following April I came home to my flat one night to find chaos down the road at the Fassaugh House pub. There had been a shooting and news was flying around the neighbourhood that it was Eamon The Don Dunne who was dead. I pulled up my hood and walked over the bridge and down the road towards the scene; it had been cordoned off and was surrounded by cops, journalists and groups of young guys. I don't know why I even went as far as I did. I knew it wasn't safe for me so I turned on my heels and went back to my flat where I watched online as details of the events emerged.

I had never been to the Fassaugh House pub, but the proximity of it to my flat and the fact it was now the scene of the latest gangland shooting in Dublin chilled me to the bone. I could easily have been spotted by Dunne or any of his cronies.

It's not that Dunne had any personal grudge against me, but everyone in the underworld would have been fine-tuned to hate me. I was the ultimate enemy of everyone: Joey The Lips, the lad who had ratted. I knew I would need to move again and this time further away.

Dunne had certainly made a name for himself since ousting Marlo. The media were linking him to anything from 10 to 17 murders and described a drug-fuelled paranoid existence towards the end. In the days after his death Dunne was described as the most powerful figure in the Irish underworld. I thought back to when he was one of Marlo's underlings; not a single thing marked him out from any of the others in the Filthy Fifty. His death reinforced one thing for me: if they want to get you they will. I knew Hinchon and Brian had access to phones and could make any arrangements they wanted, even though they were behind bars. In fact just weeks after I'd returned home, the news had featured a report that Hinchon had been caught getting drugs and mobile phones from a prison officer in Mountjoy Jail. The officer, Dillon O'Brien, was in charge of Landing B3 at the prison and brought heroin and the phone to Hinchon. He claimed he was given cocaine as payment for bringing in the contraband and he was sent to jail.

I moved again, this time further into the south city and nearer my job. I started to socialise within the gay scene and met a bloke who would become my first boyfriend. Three months after Dunne's murder, Colm Collie Owens was shot

CHAPTER 11

dead in the animal feed factory where he worked. One of the newspapers suggested a "gypsy curse" had fallen on the Filthy Fifty, leading to a series of calamities and murders, citing also the death of Anthony Anto Spratt, who had killed himself in prison just before I had given evidence in court . The story was of course a tall tale designed to flog newspapers but there was no escaping the reality. It was becoming more and more evident that a bullet in the head was just another way of doing business and I was in no doubt there was one out there with my name on it.

If I had ever been under the illusion that prison would change Brian Kenny, I was rudely awakened when I read a newspaper report in February 2011 about a court settlement involving him, his parents, Mandy and Rita Harling. To me, the report showed his determination and inability to let anything go. My jaw was literally on the ground as I read the about how they had all agreed to split the proceeds of Mitchelstown Cottage which they all claimed an interest in. Rita had actually sued Brian for her cut, and then Mandy had sued him too – presumably so Rita couldn't get the money.

If that wasn't enough, his parents, Billy and Anne, were also suing him, claiming that they had paid the mortgage for years when he was unable. It was almost comical. Brian's lawyers said he was happy to sell once each party's financial interest was recognised. The whole thing had kicked off in 2007 when Rita began legal proceedings, but the cottage was then burned to the ground and an insurance claim was paid. The report said that negotiations led to Brian receiving 40%, with 20% each going to Rita, Mandy and Brian's parents.

A couple of months later Ma rang to tell me that Rita had written a book about Brian and the awful life she'd had with him. It was called *Do Or Die, How I Escaped Life With a Murderer* by Rita Harling. That was really unexpected for me. I had no idea what had happened to Rita apart from the little I had read in the paper about the court case. I knew that the police had contacted her when I had gone to them after Jonathan's murder, and that she had told them about Brian's violent behaviour towards her. Other than that, I didn't know where she was or what had become of her. Ma picked up the book and told me a little about what was in it. It was a detailed memoir of life with Brian at Mitchelstown Cottage, and included details about me being there. I could recognise some of it, but much of it didn't make sense to me. Nonetheless I reckoned Brian would be incensed by the book, and that gave me a little bit of pleasure.

It never seemed to be long before someone I knew would either show up dead or in court, and everything would come racing home to me again. When Alan Fatpuss and Wayne Bradley were sentenced to a total of 16 years for a botched raid on a cash van, it reminded me that the past always catches up on you. Alan received a longer sentence of nine years as he played a bigger role in the raid, while Wayne, unsurprisingly, had worked as a lookout, just as he had done when Brian was working with them. When sentencing them, judge Tony Hunt said the men were part of an organised crime gang that represented "a significant evil in today's society" and said that raids were used by gangs to finance their criminal activities. He was partly right but I remain convinced that they were also carried out for a buzz, a way of getting it over on the cops and on ordinary society. During the court case an outreach worker had given evidence that Wayne had attended a "special needs" school as a kid and was pressurised into his role in the job. But the judge rejected this and said it was an insult to "special needs kids". I for one thought it was one of the funniest things I had ever read and I agreed with the judge. According to a garda who gave evidence at the trial, Alan was "second in command" to Eamon Dunne at the time, which meant he shifted loyalties very quickly after Marlo's death. I thought back to the nights when Marlo was top dog and when the Bradleys threw parties in their garden shed and everyone hollered about "Days Like This". One thing for sure was that the only loyalties in gangland were to money and power.

In Dublin I tried to stay safe but I was ultimately hiding in the lion's den. I'd avoid venues in as much as possible where I was likely to see anyone from my past, and if I visited Ma I would never tell her I was coming and climb in over the back wall. I continued to avoid all contact with former friends and family members. But Dublin is a small city and that was hammered home to me one night following an office Christmas party when one too many vodkas left me with my guard down. It must have been 1am when I stupidly went with a group from the party to a chipper in the Crumlin area which had long been a notorious crime blackspot and the scene of a decade-long feud between two warring gangs. Standing outside with my bag of chips I suddenly spotted a car out of the corner of my eye drive through a crossroads and swerve up onto a pavement near me. I sobered up in an instant and shot my head around to look straight at the driver whose eyes were almost bulging out of his head. My heart started pumping as adrenalin raced through my body, I dropped the chips and without a single word to the group I was with, I took off at a sprint up the road and into a housing estate. If I had a single doubt that Peter Joyce, Brian Kenny's now brother-in-law, had just spotted me, I was under no illusion when his car did a U-turn on the street behind me and followed me until it was stopped by a series of cement bollards marking off a cul-de-sac. I ran through a rabbit warren of streets until I thought my heart would explode in my chest. I rested briefly and then crossed to a large park which was locked up for the night. I knew the park well and scaled the wall, picking my way through the darkness to the other side. By the time I got home I was a mess.

My boyfriend had moved in and he must have noticed a rapid deterioration in my behaviour. I quickly fell into the same pattern as in England, with the half-truths, the paranoia and the real and imagined threats. My mood swings were dramatic, from extreme highs to extreme lows. I would be calm and rational and then within a short space of time I'd be up the walls but without even being able to explain why. I started hoarding again and constantly locking the doors and windows. He'd want to go out but I would refuse to walk up certain streets, cross particular bridges or even go into some shops. There was no explanation why. I'd always needed anxiety pills but I went back to the GP looking for increased doses. As before, I'd forge prescriptions and visit multiple doctors so I could self-medicate. I never touched cocaine but I would still experience chronic insomnia, a racing heart and an overwhelming paranoia about everyone and everything.

The self-doubt and hatred returned. I started questioning everything I had done and why. As my head raced I'd blame everyone around me for where I was in life. The pressure of being in a relationship started getting too much for me. Not only was I living a double life, but all the lies I was telling made me feel like I was having an affair. Even worse was the fact that I was terrified about what I was doing to my boyfriend. Every day he spent with me was one more day when he could be killed and I just couldn't live with that. He was my first proper partner and I loved him but I wouldn't have been able to live with myself if anything had happened to him. I was cruel in the end and broke his heart but I did what I had to do. He left me, no doubt confused about what I had become.

Alone again I felt like a cancer, like the dirty rat that everyone saw me as. I considered overdosing again and got as far as
rifling through a drawer to see how many tablets I could collect.
I found the dog-eared picture of Jonathan there, still attached
to the little keyring. I hadn't looked at it in a long time. What
right did I have to feel sorry for myself when he was dead? I
started to dream about him again and could picture him every
time I closed my eyes. Hinchon and Brian were locked up but
I still felt like I was being tortured by his murder.

In my turmoil I decided I'd look for him, at least what
was left of him. I found the nearest cemetery to his home in
Clondalkin and worked out how I could get there. I took two
buses and got off nearby, turning back a few times when I got
cold feet. Eventually I walked through the gates of Palmerstown
Cemetery and looked around. In front of me was a mass of
headstones and a series of concrete paths winding their way
through the vast graveyard. I walked up and down and started
reading some of the headstones, looking at the names and the
ages of those who had died. I eventually worked out that the
rows of graves were organised into years, except for where
there was a family plot.

I must have looked lost because a man on a tractor drove
towards me and beckoned for me to come closer to him. I
thought he was going to tell me to get out and that I had no
business being there, but instead he was kind. "Are you looking
for someone, son? If I can help you I will." I told him I was

CHAPTER 11

looking for the grave of Jonathan O'Reilly and I saw an immediate spark of recognition in his face. "That was the young lad that was killed outside the prison? I remember that one all right. There are some you just remember. He is over here, I'll show you." He got down off his tractor and walked ahead of me towards the back of the cemetery. Then he pointed and told me to take my time. I walked over to the grave and the first thing I saw was the same picture I had carried with me all those years. The grave was beautiful, covered in ornaments and candles.

As I read all the tributes and looked at the immaculate-ly-kept grave, tears welled up in my eyes and started to spill down my face. "I'm Joey," I said to the cold slab beneath my feet. "And I'm not doing so good." I bent down onto my hunkers and stroked the headstone, tracing my finger around the grooves which spelt out his name. I touched the photograph and the ornaments. And then I started to talk and talk and talk. I told him all about Brian Kenny and Thomas Hinchon and what they had done and how I had put them in prison and how scared I was of them. I told him how frightened I was to die in a hail of bullets just as he had. I told him about the Witness Protection Programme and about England and about coming home to Dublin and how I was really struggling to survive. For hours I wept like a baby on his graveside, and when I was finished I felt an enormous sense of peace for the first time in ages.

Every few weeks I would visit the grave, checking there was nobody there first before I would take a seat on the ground beside the headstone. I brought flowers and often left a little note written in pen. "To Jonathan, love Joey." I felt closer to that grave than I had done to any other human being in a long time. I moved flat again and started yet another job, trying hard to keep some sense of normality in my life. At night I'd toss and turn and freeze with every creak on a stairwell and every groan of a pipe. Again I seemed to be waiting to die but this time it wasn't drugs that was going to get me; it was a gunman on a promise of blood money.

Ma was very worried about me. She had contacted the Gardai on a number of occasions looking for help but had been shown the door. She had been in contact with a journalist who was writing about other people who'd been on the Witness Protection Programme but I told her I didn't want to talk. She'd also got in touch with a lawyer, who had been recommended, in the hope that he could help in some way. We were getting nowhere ourselves, doors were slamming in our faces, phones were going unanswered and anyone I had known before didn't want to know me now. I think she knew I was close to another crash but this time she wasn't sure if I would survive.

One afternoon all my fears were realised when I was walking down the Quays in Dublin city centre, my face hidden behind glasses and a hat. I could see these blokes getting animated as they walked towards me but for some reason I didn't react. Before I knew it I was on the ground getting punched and beaten. Before the first blow I had just registered one of them telling the other, "It's Joey the Lips, the fuckin' rat." I tried to protect myself but they were strong and I felt a stinging pain in my mouth. It was broad daylight but I thought I was going to be killed, right there on the ground. I went in and out of consciousness but I was aware that one of them was jumping on my head. Then there was the sound of a car horn and a flurry of activity all around me. I refused to go in the ambulance but instead took a taxi to St James's Hospital. My head hurt like hell and my lip felt like it was blowing up. The woman at the A&E department check-in looked familiar. I thought maybe she was from Ballymun. I stumbled when she asked me my name and told her I'd be back in a minute. Then I walked out the door and headed back to my flat. My lip had been stabbed my head was cut but I was more scared than anything. I'd been jumped by opportunists and not by a paid hitman. Despite being so careful about where I went, changing my routine and wearing disguises, I'd been spotted in broad daylight and I could have been killed. Simple bad luck could have sealed my fate but I also knew that my beating would be the talk of Ballymun, Finglas and beyond. It was sure to get back to the prison where Brian Kenny and Thomas Hinchon would be thirsty for revenge. But there was worse to come.

It was fast approaching the 10th anniversary of Jonathan's murder and again the Cloverhill Prison shooting was making the news. Not because Kenny and Hinchon were going into prison – rather because they were heading out. The newspaper story was devastating. Despite receiving life sentences, it revealed that Brian had already been enjoying days out to see his family and attend his son's Communion while both he and Hinchon had applied for parole. If ever I had felt the bottom falling out of my world this was it. I simply couldn't believe that Brian could have been let out or that he could even be considered for release. While it looked as if his life sentence was coming to an end, it felt like mine was only just beginning. It was such a shock to my system that he was getting to see his family. What about Jonathan's son, mother, father, sister or brother? My own daughter was growing up without a father and I hadn't see her on her Communion day like Brian had. All I had was a picture in a frame given to me by her grandmother.

Days later I was sitting on the banks of the canal in Dublin being interviewed by the journalist who had spoken to Ma. Dressed in my bullet proof vest I told her what had happened to me. "I don't know where to turn. I'm frightened that I'm going to be killed. I've been of use to the state but I'm not anymore. I've been hung out to dry," I said. "You hear about this murder and that murder and the gardai looking for witnesses to come forward. I came forward. I put away the bad guys and look how I've ended up. My life is totally destroyed. I look over my shoulder everywhere I go. I don't want to die but I'm being left destitute. They've hung me out to dry."

Later I went to the offices of the Department of Justice where I was told that the then Minister Francis Fitzgerald wasn't available to talk to me. The article ran on the front page of the paper but still I heard nothing except for a brief call with a politician who vowed to pursue my case with the appropriate authorities. The silence was deafening and it seemed that absolutely nobody cared.

I wrote to the Garda Commissioner and told her about my concerns about the therapy that was provided for me while I was on the Programme, and the nature of my exit from it so soon after my suicide attempt. Other aspects of how I was signed off appeared to me to be worthy of an independent investigation by the Garda Síochána and I indicated my willingness to co-operate. I received no response. I also made a complaint to the Garda Síochána Ombudsman Commission who carried out some preliminary enquiries, but then never came back to me. I really felt worthless, like I had no voice or nothing of importance to say.

But then something amazing happened, something that remains one of the best things that has ever occurred in my life. Through a series of complex arrangements Delores O'Reilly, Jonathan's mother, was put in touch with Ma. She had been gutted to read about what had happened to me. She told Ma that she had always imagined that I'd disappeared into the sunset and that I'd be sipping cocktails on a sun-kissed beach until I grew old. The miserable truth of what had happened to my life had knocked her for six and despite all the rules and the regulations, she wanted to meet me and to thank me for what I had done. We decided that Ma would meet her first and then we'd decide what I would do. The two of them hit it off immediately. In a way both of them had lost their sons even though I was still alive. After more complex planning it was arranged for me to meet her.

The minute I walked into her house I felt as if I'd come home. Delores was warm and strong. She embraced me and told me over and over again how grateful she was for what I'd done. She must have held me to her for at least half an hour. "You haven't changed a bit. You still look like a little young fella," she told me, but I knew that inside I had changed. Photographs of Jonathan adorned the walls of the house and along the sideboard. They showed him as he grew from child to man and some showed him with his little son Kyle, who'd been left fatherless by Brian and Hinchon's decision to play God. It was so lovely to be thanked and to hear from the family that I had made a difference to their lives. I told her that I had always dreamed about Jonathan and about going to the grave and finding some peace there. She was amazed. She said she always wondered who had left the flowers there. She had often phoned around family members and friends to ask who had left them, with a note that had always been washed clean by rain or morning dew. I had always been afraid they would catch me there at the grave and I worried they'd think I was an imposter. I needn't have, because from the minute I walked into their home I felt like I belonged.

Days later Delores did an interview with a newspaper describing how she and her family had met me and how horrified they were at the way I had been treated. "For so long I wanted to meet this man. I was hurt I could not speak to him. I just wanted to thank him for being so brave and give him a hug because only for him we would not have got justice," she told the journalist. "So I finally met him, but it took 11 years and I thanked him and gave him that big hug. For more than a decade, I was under the impression that this wonderful young man that I never knew but held close to my heart was living a safe and secure and happy life somewhere abroad, and that he had been given a second chance having single handily put two murderers behind bars when he was only a child. I am now absolutely devastated that that was not the case; it didn't even come close to the idea I had. He got justice for my son Jonathan, and this is the thanks he gets. He was beaten and abused by Brian Kenny, made errands carrying heroin for him and Thomas Hinchon and he was totally controlled by both of them and lived in terror. He led the police to the gun that was used to kill my son; he stood in the witness box at only 19 and was a prize possession for the Gardai who got a safe and secure conviction for these two dangerous men. But while we could go home to our houses in the safe knowledge that Kenny and Hinchon were put away for life, and believing Joey was given a whole new life as a reward for his outstanding bravery, we are now shattered having learned that the past decade for Joey has been hell on earth. He has been completely and utterly let down by the state and we feel while we have lost our son, and we miss him beyond words, there is guilt now in our home because we find ourselves questioning if Joey did the right thing at all given the awful life he has lived since. While Joey has reassured us time and time again that he has no regrets and he is more than happy with standing up to both of those murderers, we feel terribly guilty that he never received any rewards for what he has done for us and for the state. Instead of being decorated for his bravery, he has been thrown in a skip of hell. I am determined more than ever to never let these animals Kenny and Hinchon see the light of day and I will stand with Joey and his mother Mary in our quest to keep them behind bars. I'll do all that I can to make this happen. I now know the full and shocking extent of how Kenny in particular ruined that man's life, and he is evil beyond words. We have all written letters to the relevant people and we will fight until the end to keep those men locked away."

Delores and the rest of Jonathan's family were true to their word and later, when a parole board met to consider applications for the release of Kenny and Hinchon, they were met with a raft of letters of objection by the O'Reilly's, Ma and me. Both the requests were turned down and we were all able to gasp for breath before having to get up to fight again. But while I had gained a family from my experience and had grown stronger with their love, there were still many parts of me that were broken. If I was to survive my past, I knew that I needed to fix my future. It was time for me and Ma to take one last journey on our own.

Convicted killer Brian Kenny on day release to hospital in 2018.

CHAPTER 12

They say it's a small world and I can certainly attest to that. My life seems to have moved in a series of scenes, with characters from some episodes returning when least expected. At Dublin Airport one particular character made a dramatic comeback at the most inopportune moment. I had been getting more and more unwell since the news of Brian Kenny's days out from prison to see his family. It seemed so terribly unfair to me that he was still winning and despite the fact that I had sacrificed everything to give evidence against him, he was still able to play the system and enjoy things that I couldn't. I had become more and more paranoid at the thought of the power he wielded, even behind bars, and the idea that he could be out of prison without me even knowing it. I would spend nights awake looking out the spyhole, locking and relocking my doors and windows, pacing the floors and reliving the beatings and rapes over and over again. Inside my head I was being tortured, tormented by my past and unclear about my future. In an effort to sleep I was self-medicating again, with Valium and huge doses of anti-anxiety pills. Every time I contacted the Gardai I was shown the door and told to go back to England but that certainly wasn't an option for me. Their attitude was cruel, especially to someone in my condition. At one point a meeting was set up with a Garda in a car park outside the city. When arrived, I sat in his car thinking he was going to help me but he had been sent by Witness Protection to tell me they were finished with me. "Can you understand this? You need to fuck off. We are done with you. You did your deal," he said. Each rejection hit harder and in my head I felt stupid and used and lied to all over again.

A psychologist I had been seeing since I first returned to Ireland and detoxed was absolutely amazing. She recognised how unwell I was and was very worried about me. She had been working with me for years and trying to help me avoid triggers and to stay clean but she could see the turmoil I was in. She knew my story and was watching the reality of my situation playing out on the news. As my health deteriorated she told me straight out that if I didn't get help I would die. "I can't see you lasting much longer," she told me one day as I shook and cried in her office. She told me I was suffering a full mental breakdown and that the treatment I needed was so intense it wasn't even available in Ireland. She mentioned the Priory Clinic in the UK where she said I would benefit hugely from residential care. I hadn't the money and had no hope in raising it so help seemed even further away than ever. But the lawyer my Ma had found was a really good guy and was talking to the cops. After a letter from the psychologist, he set up a meeting with a very senior officer. Somehow he had finally got through to them.

The officer agreed that the Garda Síochána would pay for my treatment and in March 2016, at my lowest ebb, I found myself flanked by two officers at Dublin Airport saying an emotional goodbye to Ma yet again. She was so worried about me that she didn't want to let me go and asked if she could walk with me to the security gate. She then spotted Rita Harling checking bags and patting down passengers heading into the departures lounges. Neither Ma nor I had seen Rita since she was living with Brian. The sight of her literally stopped us in our tracks. Every way we turned it seemed there was a reminder of Brian Kenny and his influence over people. The cops that were with me turned me around and used their badges to get us through a different part of the airport and to the departure gate for my flight to the UK. I couldn't even speak. It felt like my entire system was shutting down. I felt humiliated, timid, frail and sick.

In Wales we met two big policemen who were nice and shook my hand. I was taken to a hotel conference room where I sat in the corner waiting for the people from the Priory to come and get me. Eventually there was a knock on the door and a woman in her mid-60s walked in and introduced herself as Angela. She looked around. "Which one is Joseph?" I lifted my head. "Right I will take it from here," she said and picked up my bags. On the way to her car she told me that she had been led to believe that I was some big gangster but that one look at me had told her I wasn't. We laughed and I relaxed a little bit.

The centre was up in the mountains and was reached by a magnificent long driveway. We made our way past a big grey building which Angela told me was the hospital for people who had been sectioned. We drove on towards a newer building of four bedrooms: my home for the foreseeable future. A hot dinner was waiting for me and Angela showed me to my room which was lovely and clean. I was totally exhausted, both mentally and physically and that night when I hit the bed, I actually slept for the first time in weeks.

Straight away there was a plan and a structure for me. After a few days of rest my sessions started, and for the first four weeks I wasn't allowed speak to my family. The staff reassured me that they would phone Ma and let her know how I was getting on and that she could contact them whenever she wished. I had three different therapy sessions a day with a psychologist, a counsellor and a psychiatrist who first took me off all my medication and then assessed me. My diagnosis was crushing. I had Post Traumatic Stress Disorder, Obsessive Compulsive Disorder and Bipolar and Anxiety Disorder. I hadn't been born with any of these, but they could each be traced back to the psychological effects of living with Brian.

CHAPTER 12

After the first month I was slowly placed back on medication which was carefully monitored in order to treat my
disorders. They explained I would need these medications for
the rest of my life, like anyone with a mental health illness. My
addiction to Benzos would have to continue as I needed them
to stay well. It took me a while to get used to that and to accept
how unwell I am mentally, but once I realised how well they
worked, I began to feel so much better. I'm still on 15 tablets
a day and will be for the rest of my life. They slow down my
thoughts, stabilise my mood and help stop the nightmares, but
most importantly they make me feel well.

The routine was good for me. I would get up every
morning at 8.30am, shower and shave and make my breakfast. Then I would go to the gym and be in my first session
by mid-morning. It was quite strange in the beginning. They
wanted to know my story but they didn't want me to dwell on
the past, they just wanted me to talk about my current feelings.
I suppose they deconstructed me and then built me back up
brick by brick. I'd rage about the Gardai and how they had
treated me but they would make me see that I needed to take
control of the situation. I had a habit of saying "I had to" do
something because I had been told to do so; they made me see
how that was all related to Brian's control over me and how it
had continued to affect all the other relationships in my life.

We talked about my relationship with my Da and with Brian,
although we weren't allowed to mention his name because he

had abused me. I'd get all worked up about him saying he was still winning, but Angela gradually helped me see that he wasn't. While he was able to leave prison to see his family, he always had to return to the confinement of his cell. They gave me methods to ease his mental power over me; although he was locked up he continued to control me through the fear I had of him. They told me that Brian was a bully and a murderer and Angela, who had worked in prisons for much of her career, described him as a psychopath.

She told me that Brian's treatment of me was classic psychopathic behaviour. She said he picked me because of my good qualities and my vulnerabilities but pointed out that he hadn't been so smart because he had picked the wrong guy. She said I'd been clever enough to destroy everything that he and Hinchon had been building. Despite them having all the money and the drugs and being so powerful, the truth was that I had destroyed both of them. I buried the gun and burned their leathers in places no one else would be able to find. And then when I gave up the evidence to the Gardai I had left them with no options. "You have to remember he is lying there in his cell and he has been done over by a young lad," she told me. She described how Kenny had pushed and pushed me mentally, through the beatings and the rapes, and that in the end I had become so numb I couldn't feel anything anymore. That was his downfall; I had been able to move against him because my feelings had been shut down.

I think Brian had seen my vulnerability when he first met me. He made me feel special. He had eight boys working for him but he made me his number one. I was his best boy, his fastest, his hardest worker. He trusted me and gave me the money to look after, the milk to collect and the praise that I just lapped up. For my part I had seen a lot of hardship and I wanted to provide for my family, for Ma and the girls. I wanted a father figure and Brian abused that position as well. He controlled me with fear and with mind games, threatening me with guns and all the rest. He became a monster for me the night he beat Jessie with the hammer. I spent every minute of every day thereafter trying to keep away from that monster. I remain convinced that was the trigger for the PTSD.

The emotional work and the psychological stuff was absolutely amazing and I could feel myself getting better every day. With the counsellor I explored my emotions and my relationships with my family, and even with my partner John who had left me without knowing who I really was. Being able to talk without being afraid was absolutely amazing for me. Some days I would just sit in the room and I'd be scared. Sometimes I would cry for the hour but it was liberating for me to let all that out. It seemed I had always been told what to do and what to say and that I had spent my life being told to "shut up". In the safety of such a caring environment I was finally able to talk and cry and rage and for the first time it wasn't all bottled up in my own head.

Of course the biggest relationship in my life was with my Ma and because we had been through so much together we were incredibly close. We had still somehow managed to lose one another along the way and they wanted to identify where that happened so they could repair it. I remember Angela saying to me that if we could figure out where we had got lost, we could heal. It was, of course, the time when Brian Kenny came along and when I had started lying to her. Ma felt enormously guilty that she hadn't looked after me properly and that was why I had gone off with Brian. I had to admit I had lied to her to convince her I was living a happy life with Brian and that we were just doing ordinary work.

Ma had been nervous about me going to Wales. I think she was scared of losing me again but she also believed in me so much that she knew all I ever needed was the opportunity to receive the right sort of help and I'd grab it with both hands. After a while Ma came to see me and was blown away by the difference in me. She was angry too. She could see how well I had become in such a short time and she knew that if Witness Protection had looked after me properly I wouldn't have lost 10 years off my life. Ma had therapy too, first on her own. Then we did it together. I told her all that I had been through with Brian, even the difficult details about the rapes. Ma was broken herself: she felt so guilty; she felt she had let me down and that everything was her fault. We talked about what me Da had put her through and how we had lost one another when Brian came along. I took responsibility for my faults and admitted I had lied to her to convince her everything was okay when I was living with him. I told her I had only done it to keep her and the family safe. I had just felt trapped; I had got in too deep before I really knew what was happening. Ma came every few weeks to see me and we'd do our therapy and go for dinner. I was getting stronger all the time and she'd tell me how proud she was of me. She still tells me that now. Every single time we talk.

On a practical level I also started to learn life skills at the Priory. It may sound simple but having a routine, like washing clothes, making beds and cooking a meal is all very important to mental health. I also had the paranoia and the fear to deal with. My Obsessive Compulsive Disorder had fed that fear in a particular way. I was a slave to locking doors, checking spy-holes and minding my security. While I clearly had to be much more security-minded than most, I had to learn how to be practical about it and not let it take over my life.

That aspect of my mental illness, particularly the stockpiling, can be really strange . I remember when I was at the Priory I had a bit of an attack of it and had been stashing air fresheners. They raided my room one morning and took boxes of them away. While collecting such a peculiar item is undoubtedly funny, it is a manifestation of my mind irrationally preparing for the worst, getting ready for a war. The fact that I was going into battle with a hundred lavender-smelling pellets is really not the issue: it is the utter lack of logic and control that is.

We discussed the Witness Protection Programme at length and how it became another prison for me where I was again being controlled. The therapy I was offered on the Programme was not what I needed and in fact the staff at the Priory were shocked by it. I had needed proper psychiatric help but I hadn't received anything like that.

The way I was signed off the Programme remains an absolute disgrace. I was ripped away from my child, my family and everything I knew – like that sticking plaster effect. But it was at a time I was at my most vulnerable. Most people go into the Witness Protection Programme to save their own skin but I went to the garda to do the right thing. They didn't do right by me and I lost everything all over again.

I made huge steps at the Priory. I will never forget the first time I walked down the mountain road on my own to the little village below to have a cup of coffee. It was the first time I had felt peace and when a car could pass me without my heart starting to race. For most people that might seem like a normal thing, but when your mind is being irrational, a simple trip to a coffee shop can cause more anxiety than you would believe.

Half way through my programme I received devastating news. Ma had been involved in an accident back in Ireland and in hospital they realised that she had suffered a brain aneurysm and was very seriously ill. The staff were very worried about me and thought I would fall apart; I was able to speak to her on the phone and she made me promise to stick with it. "Joseph, no matter what happens to me I want you to promise me that you will finish this and that you will get well. Promise me," she whispered down the phone. And I did. I swore I wouldn't walk out and that I would keep going and that I would see her soon. Thankfully she recovered from the operation.

My battle continues to this day. That battle is to survive and to forgive myself. I'm a fighter and I have a "never say die" attitude to life. But I know that despite all I have done in my past, I am a good and honest person. I am caring, hard-working and I have compassion for others. I have very strong morals when it comes to right and wrong and I have the best Ma in all the world. She isn't only my Ma, she is my bodyguard and my biggest supporter. When the world turned against me, she was there for me. I'd give everything I have to her because I know she'd never do anything without thinking about me first. She has been in a relationship for the last 20 years and Denis is an absolute rock too. He has been very good to me and has always provided sound and thoughtful advice. We all need people like that in our lives.

It is absolute nonsense that being a rat is the greatest sin in all of gangland . Most people involved in crime are ratting on one another all the time anyway. They rob one another, go off with each other's wives and have absolutely no loyalty to anyone or anything. For years I have read in the papers about people I know calling for witnesses to come forward when it's their loved ones who have taken a bullet. These are the same ones who called me a rat, so where is the sense in that? People in glasshouses shouldn't throw stones.

Despite everything, my moral code never changed. The shame I felt selling drugs was awful. I used to pray at night that the junkies wouldn't overdose. I don't think I fitted into the underworld but I think I ended up in it because I was scared and pliable. But after the murder I knew it was my time to check out.

Nowadays when I get up each day I check my cameras to see what's been going on while I was sleeping and I plan my daily routine to precision so I can safely get from A to B. I do other practical things like making sure my phones are charged and I have my alarm on me all the time. I have a good relationship with the police where I live now and I know I can call on them any time. They often drop in to visit and to make sure everything is alright.

I work to pay the bills and I try to keep myself fit and healthy. I hope to stay clean and continue minding my mental health. If I had three wishes they would be simple: for my family and children to be safe, well and healthy, for my career to grow and to settle down one day with someone who accepts me for me.

The nightmares don't come as frequently now but I still sense them sometimes in the darkness. I feel the clawing fingers on my covers, the hands around my throat. When I wake up I thank God for another day. I pray to Jonathan and thank him for protecting me. Until the day I die I will do everything in my power to keep his killers in jail. As long as I have breath in me I'll never stop fighting to keep them locked up.

Letter to parole board dated May 8 2019

My name is Joseph O'Callaghan and I am writing to you about Brian Kenny who I understand has applied for parole. I understand that this letter will be given to Brian Kenny so I have to be careful in regards to what I write, but I will try my best to articulate my feelings.

As a result of Brian Kenny's actions I was signed on to the State's Witness Protection Programme at the age of just 19. I was the youngest person ever to be placed on the programme and found it extremely difficult and life changing.

Up until that point I had lived with Brian Kenny after first working for him at the age of 12.

When I moved in with Brian Kenny I thought I had found some sanctuary but instead I found myself embroiled and trapped in a far worse place.

As a child Brian Kenny taught me to steal, to take drugs and to sell heroin. Through fear and the control he had over me I literally become a slave to him. Looking back now I can see how I was groomed by him for his own selfish ends but at the time I didn't have the maturity to realise what was happening to me so I went along with it.

I was regularly beaten by Mr Kenny and raped. He used the sexual violence as part of his control over me which was all-encompassing. I felt I had nowhere to turn at the time and so I learned the ways of his world and I did things out of a paralysing fear of him.

In April 2004 Brian Kenny and his partner Thomas Hinchon planned and carried out the murder of Jonathan O'Reilly whom they shot dead outside Cloverhill Prison. I never knew Jonathan but he was only 24 and with his whole life ahead of him. When they asked me to get rid of the evidence of his murder I couldn't do it. Jonathan was not much older than me and I was terrified of their capabilities and how they had so easily ended a life.

I was frightened and I ran to my mother for the first time in years.

Together we decided that I had to do what was right and so we went to the Gardai and I told them what Brian Kenny and Thomas Hinchon had done. I told them where to find the gun they had used and the getaway bike. From that moment I signed away my own life. In my case, my sentence actually means life and I have no option to apply for parole.

The fallout from my decision to do the right thing will live with me and my loved ones forever.

CHAPTER 12

Both Brian Kenny and Thomas Hinchon were convicted of murder and I gave evidence against them convinced that they would be locked up appropriately. In my mind taking someone else's life is the worst thing any human being can do to another and I think it should be punishable accordingly. In giving evidence I hoped they would never be a danger to me or those I loved again. But I was wrong.

Since that day in 2004 I have been forced to live under an assumed identity and in hiding. I cannot see my family or any of my old friends. I am alone in the world and I am still very, very scared. I know that one day Brian Kenny will come and get his revenge on me. I have constant nightmares that he will get out of prison and come after me.

Even behind bars Brian Kenny threatens me, often sending his cohorts out to try to find out where I am and threatening my family. I was badly beaten once on a visit back to Dublin and my mother's home has been smashed up. Amongst other things I suffer from extreme Post Traumatic Stress Disorder as a result of Brian Kenny's actions and the fear I still have of him.

I fear that he is hell-bent on getting back at me for giving evidence against him and I know that he blames me completely for his incarceration. He has taken no responsibility whatsoever for the choices he made to take Jonathan O'Reilly's life from him. Instead he continues to terrorise me and my family for speaking the truth about him. I was informed only a few months ago that Brian Kenny had offered money to someone to have me killed. He will stop at nothing to get back at me and setting him free would be akin to signing my death warrant. I believed in the system of justice when I told the truth and gave evidence in court. I believed that when Brian Kenny was given a life sentence that meant that he would not be considered for parole after such a short length of time.

Jonathan O'Reilly is not here to tell anyone how he feels about Brian Kenny seeking his liberty. But I am and I want to leave you in no doubt that I object to this parole application in the strongest possible terms. I beg you not to let him out of prison. The hurt he has caused for so many people is only eased because he is in jail. I would feel completely let down by the state and justice if Brian Kenny was to be freed at this point in time. While I cannot speak for Jonathan O'Reilly I believe that he would feel the same.

Yours.

Joseph O'Callaghan

Acknowledgements

I would like to thank Nicola and all at Mirror Books for believing in my story and handling it so sensitively. Writing a book is a huge achievement for me and I hope it will show others that there is another way. To Kieran, a top-class gentleman and brilliant lawyer who has helped me so much. I would like to thank my counsellor Peter, my psychiatrist Dr Rooney, Angela and all the staff in the Priory Clinic for helping me become the man I am today. I can never thank you all enough.

Joseph O'Callaghan

There are so many stories and too many victims when it comes to reporting on gangland crime. But one has always stood out for me and that is the story of Joey 'The Lips' O'Callaghan. I hope I have done it justice and lifted a lid on a dark place we should all know a little bit about, because sometimes if you look you can find decent human beings there trapped in an evil place. This is Joey's story and now is his time. Thank you Jo Sollis and all at Mirror books.

Nicola Tallant